BE TRANSFORMED

Letting the Spirit Renew Your Mind

By Karen Baney

*Do not conform to the pattern of this world, but **be transformed by the renewing of your mind**. Then you will be able to test and approve what God's will is—his good, pleasing and perfect will.*

—Romans 12:2 NIV

Be Transformed: Letting the Spirit Renew Your Mind
By Karen Baney

Copyright © 2018, 2021 by Karen Baney
Cover Design by Brian Ring Designs

ISBN 978-0-9855862-8-7

Printed in the United States of America
Author Services International, LLC
3281 E Joseph Way
Gilbert, AZ 85295
www.karenbaney.com

TABLE OF CONTENTS

For the past few years, I have been on a journey to change my thinking. I had no choice. My thought patterns were hurting me, my family, and my career.

At a very young age, I accepted Christ as my Lord and Savior and, other than a few years in my early twenties, I spent my entire life following Jesus. Nevertheless, when life seemed to bring problem after problem, I grew frustrated and discontent.

My faith was not making a difference or a dent in the chaos that was my life. Why couldn't I experience the contentment or joy that was supposed to come with the Christian life?

So, I asked God this question and He slowly began revealing to me that my thinking was toxic and unhealthy. It was the root cause of most of my inner turmoil. It was why I felt like I had no victory even though I had been saved.

I wish I could tell you that the transformation of my thoughts happened overnight. I wish I could tell you that in a matter of months I was totally different. This journey for me started about six years ago and it continues to be a daily choice.

The first revelation came when I learned that <u>I was the problem</u> and that <u>my thinking was the source</u>. Then I had to take very repetitive and deliberate steps to start thinking about my thought patterns. Then I learned that this transformation required time and commitment and even some counseling.

After the initial year, I started to feel like I was losing some ground for which I had fought valiantly. I began reading and listening to every book and Bible study I could get my hands on related to changing my thinking. I put into practice what the Word said about the topic. I prayed, cried, journaled, studied, and talked to friends and my husband. I was determined to never go back to my old way of thinking.

Sometimes a book or Bible study would help prompt a significant "ah-ha" moment where the Spirit unlocked an old truth for me in a way that it just made sense. Sometimes the Spirit simply reminded me to persevere.

So, as you get ready to walk with me through the next seven weeks, I want to leave you with these parting thoughts about what transformation looks like.

Take the butterfly, for example. It begins life as a fluffy, not-so-pretty caterpillar. Every day moves it closer to becoming a beautiful butterfly.

My old way of thinking was ugly just like the caterpillar. However, as I kept working on my thinking, I eventually came to a time where my new thought patterns, based on God's Word, acted like a cocoon. It insulated my heart and protected it while the hardest part of the Spirit's work took place. Then one day, I woke up and wondered when I had become such a beautiful butterfly with transformation written all over my thought life.

I don't know where you are in your journey but take heart. The Spirit is alive in you if you know Christ and He is helping you transform by the renewing of your mind.

Blessings,

Karen

Online resources available:

www.karenbaney.com/be-transformed

- Leader Guide
- Session Answers

Do not conform to the pattern of this world, but be transformed by the renewing of your mind. Then you will be able to test and approve what God's will is—his good, pleasing and perfect will. –Romans 12:2

OUR MIND, HEART, AND THOUGHTS MATTER TO GOD

There are over _____ references to the word _____

in the Bible.

God _____ knows our: (Psalm 139:1-4, 23-24)

- • _____ (v2)

- • _____ before they are _____ (v4)

- • _____ (v23,24)

We _____ out of what is _____ _____ in

our _____. (Matt. 12:33-35)

(Our actions flow from our words which flow from our hearts.)

We are _____ for our _____.
(Matt. 12:36-37)

Our human nature cannot be _____ because we

_____ ourselves. (Jeremiah 17:9)

THE WORLD'S WAY

"Do not conform to the pattern of this world..."

The _____ way to renewing our minds relies solely

on _____.

- Stuff emotions
- Ignore thoughts
- Deny we have a problem
- Sheer will & determination

GOD'S WAY

"...but be transformed by the renewing of your mind..."

STRANGE PARTNERSHIP

"Be transformed" _____ that we are _____

_____ in the transformation process.

The Spirit is _____ and that same _____

_____ in us! (Rom. 8:11, Eph. 1:13-14)

The Spirit will _____ you of _____

thinking when you do your part to learn about yourself and

_____ your _____. (John 14:26)

LASTING CHANGE

"...Then you will be able to test and approve what God's will is—his good, pleasing and perfect will."

Choosing God's Way yields a dividend of _____

and _____.

_____

_____

_____

_____

_____

_____

Our thoughts about ourselves, others, and even God, can affect our lives in so many ways. Our thoughts can harm our relationships. They can harm our view of God's character or obscure our understanding of Him and His love for us. They can turn into negative actions like a loss of self-control, emotional outbursts, foolish choices, and so much more.

When I first started this journey to change how and what I think, I had to first understand that I could change. Then I had to learn how to recognize my thought patterns.

In my marriage, I had established some very negative thought patterns. I used to think that when my husband was very quiet it was because he was mad at me. And from that thought, I would start an argument because I thought it wasn't fair for him to be angry at me and not tell me why. Through much personal growth, I finally listened to him when he said that he wasn't angry at all. He just had nothing to say.

You can change your thought patterns

So where do we begin our journey to change our thought patterns? First, we must understand and believe that we *can* change our thinking. Second, we must practice changing our thoughts. We will tackle both things this week by looking at scripture, praying, and journaling.

Our theme verse for this study comes from Romans 12:2 in the NIV and is listed on the title page of this workbook for easy reference. I encourage you to memorize this verse during the study.

> *Do not conform to the pattern of this world, but be transformed by the renewing of your mind. Then you will be able to test and approve what God's will is—his good, pleasing and perfect will. —Romans 12:2 NIV*

Remember to highlight, star, or mark any verses or ideas that speak to you this week. We will use them for an activity during the last week.

DAY 1: YOU CAN CHANGE

One of the most profound moments in my journey to change my thinking and renew my mind was when I learned that I could truly change my thinking. I was not a slave to every thought that popped into my mind or every emotion that I felt. I could choose to act on it or not.

IN THE FOLLOWING VERSE, CIRCLE "BE TRANSFORMED". UNDERLINE THE PART OF THE VERSE THAT TELLS HOW WE ARE TO BE TRANSFORMED.

Do not conform to the pattern of this world, but be transformed by the renewing of your mind. Then you will be able to test and approve what God's will is—his good, pleasing and perfect will.

–Romans 12:2 NIV

WHAT DOES "TRANSFORMED" MEAN?

DO YOU THINK THAT GOD'S WORD WOULD TELL US TO BE SOMETHING, LIKE "BE TRANSFORMED", IF IT WAS NOT POSSIBLE FOR US TO CHANGE? WHY OR WHY NOT?

That was the question that rolled around in my mind in the earliest part of my journey. I firmly believe that when God's Word tells us to do something, like "be transformed" or "put off", or "put on", we are capable and empowered by His Spirit to do those things.

WHAT AND HOW TO CHANGE

The following verses tell us what we need to change in our thinking and in our hearts. They also tell us how to change.

FILL IN THE BLANKS FOR THE FOLLOWING VERSES (NIV VERSION). PAY ATTENTION TO THE BOLDED PHRASES IN EACH VERSE.

_____ your _____ **on things above**, not on earthly things. –Colossians 3:2

[22]You were taught, with regard to your former way of life, to _____ _____ your **old self**, which is being corrupted by its deceitful desires; [23]to _____ _____ _____ in the **attitude of your minds**; [24]and to _____ _____ the **new self**, created to be like God in true righteousness and holiness.

–Ephesians 4:22-24

_____ these _____ of mine **in your hearts and minds**; _____ them as symbols **on your hands** and _____ them **on your foreheads**. –Deuteronomy 11:18

_____ **in the Lord with all your heart** and _____ _____ **on your own understanding; in all your ways** _____ to _____, and he will make your paths straight. –Proverbs 3:5-6

FOLLOW THE EXAMPLE BELOW AND WRITE DOWN ALL THE WORDS YOU WROTE ON THE BLANKS IN THE FIRST COLUMN. THEN WRITE ALL OF THE BOLDED WORDS IN THE SECOND COLUMN.

Example (Colossians 3:2): Set your mind – on things above

Filled In Words ("How" we change / action we take)	Bolded Words (the "What" / object of our action)
Set your mind	On things above

Week 1: Changing Thought Patterns

PICK ONE OF THE VERSES FROM TODAY'S LESSON AND PERSONALIZE IT BY REPLACING ANY "YOU", "YOUR" TYPE WORDS WITH "I", "ME", AND "MY".

Example using Romans 12:2:

> I will not conform to the pattern of this world, but I will be transformed by the renewing of my mind. Then I will be able to test and approve what God's will is—his good, pleasing and perfect will.

When we personalize scripture in this way, it helps us remember what the verse says, and it helps us start to see how we can apply it to our lives.

Throughout the rest of this study we will learn ways to set our minds on things above and how to fix God's word in our hearts and minds. I hope today's lesson opened your mind and heart to see that you can change your thought patterns and that it gave you a glimpse of how the change can take place.

Several times a year, my husband and I go to our favorite restaurant for Sunday brunch. It is a very popular place in the winter time, due to Phoenix's great winter weather, so we usually make a reservation.

One day when we arrived, the wait was more than one hour. We had reserved a table, so we zipped past the long line and were seated immediately. However, we were still close enough to the hostess stand to hear one gentleman cursing loudly and talking down to the hostess. He was very upset about the long wait and, even though he had not made a reservation, he expected to be seated immediately. His words made it clear that he felt he deserved something better than the other customers who had been waiting longer.

Our words reveal a lot about us and they are one tool we can use to help us change our thought patterns.

OUR WORDS FLOW FROM OUR THOUGHTS

In Matthew 15:1-20, Jesus encounters some Pharisees who are angry because Jesus's disciples did not complete ritual hand washing prior to eating food. (The Pharisee tradition was to wash their hands prior to eating so they would not become defiled by the food they ate.) Jesus calls them out because they placed more value on their traditions than they did on the Word of God.

READ MATTHEW 15:11, 17-20. ACCORDING TO JESUS IN VERSE 11, WHAT DEFILES A PERSON?

WHERE DO OUR WORDS COME FROM (V18)?

We may not think murderous thoughts, though what our heart or mind dwells on impacts what we say. Our thoughts direct our words. And our words have consequences.

For many years, I used to think that every time I went to the gym, everyone was staring at me. I was extremely self-conscious, and this thought pattern created a great deal of anxiety in my life. One day I expressed this thought out loud to my husband by saying that I hated going to the gym because everyone staring at me makes me feel bad about myself. He set me straight by telling me that no one thinks about me nearly as much as I think they do. At the time, I didn't agree, and I stopped going to the gym because I couldn't deal with the stress—which I created with my own thoughts!

READ THE FOLLOWING VERSES. NOTE WHAT TYPE OF WORDS THE VERSE IS TALKING ABOUT. THEN LIST THE CONSEQUENCE. IN SOME CASES, THERE MAY BE MORE THAN ONE.

Verse	Type of Words	Consequences
PROVERBS 12:18	Reckless words Wise words	Hurt others Heal
PROVERBS 15:1		
PROVERBS 17:9		
PROVERBS 18:6		
PROVERBS 18:19		
PROVERBS 18:21		
PROVERBS 20:19		

When we take the time to stop and evaluate the words we speak, we can learn to identify what is going on in our hearts. Had I examined the reason behind why I felt like everyone was staring at me at the gym, I would have discovered what was going on in my heart: I was feeling extremely insecure about myself and I had been saying very negative things to myself about my body (negative self-talk).

WRITE PROVERBS 20:27 BELOW.

God's Word also helps shed light on what is going on in our hearts. When we read the Bible, the Holy Spirit will cause words to jump off the page at us. Those are things He is prompting us to stop and take a closer look at. Maybe there is something going on in our hearts that we need to adjust.

PICK ONE OF THE VERSES FROM TODAY'S LESSON AND PERSONALIZE IT BY REPLACING ANY "YOU", "YOUR" TYPE WORDS WITH "I", "ME", AND "MY".

DAY 3: ACTIONS

"Actions speak louder than words." –Anonymous

From Session 1, when we studied Matthew 12:33-37, we learned that our actions flow from our words which flow from our thoughts. Our actions towards others communicates loud and clear what we really think about them. The same is true of how we treat ourselves.

OUR ACTIONS FOLLOW OUR THOUGHTS

After shopping for new clothes, I hid the receipt from my husband even though I stayed within the budget. I did it because I was afraid my husband would be mad at me. Not once had he ever been upset in the past, but I still approached him with doubt and fear. My husband never did anything to warrant my behavior.

The doubt, fear, and guilt I felt over doing *nothing wrong* stemmed entirely from my thoughts. I believed that if I were a good wife, I would be more frugal. I could have found more discounts and made that money go farther.

My warped thoughts about myself and my faulty beliefs about what a good wife did or didn't do resulted in me hiding the receipt and caused me to feel unwarranted fear, guilt, and shame.

READ JAMES 1:13 – 15. WHAT CAN WE LEARN ABOUT TEMPTATION FROM THESE VERSES?

WHAT IS A DESIRE? IS IT AN EMOTION? IS IT A THOUGHT? OR BOTH ACCORDING TO THESE VERSES?

WHAT DOES DESIRE GIVE BIRTH TO?

Desire starts in our heart as a thought and, if left unchecked, it leads to an action (sin).

READ 2 SAMUEL 11:1-4. WHERE WAS DAVID AND WHAT WAS HE DOING?

WHAT DID DAVID SEE?

WHAT DID DAVID DO AFTER HE SAW?

WHERE DID DAVID'S SIN BEGIN?

David's sin began with a thought. He saw a beautiful woman. Then he thought about her until desire gave way to lust and lust gave way to adultery. If we read the rest of the story (2 Samuel 11:5 - 12:19), we see that the consequences of David's lustful thought, followed by his action of infidelity, eventually led him to murder Bathsheba's husband, and to cover it up. This finally led to the death of the baby Bathsheba had conceived.

WHAT COULD DAVID HAVE DONE DIFFERENTLY TO STOP HIS DESIRE FROM "CONCEIVING AND GIVING BIRTH TO SIN"?

Best case, David could have stopped his path of sin right at the beginning with his thoughts. When he saw Bathsheba bathing on her roof, he could have gone inside his room and read a book or sang a song or just gone to bed alone.

Even if David went beyond the initial thought, he had the ability to stop before committing adultery. He also had the ability to stop and confess to his friend (Bathsheba's husband) instead of killing him. He could have chosen to not cover up the murder.

There were so many points along the way where David could have made a better choice.

The same is true of us. We don't have to give into to every thought that pops into our mind. We can choose not to act on that thought. We can choose to change our scenery or call a friend or pray.

READ JOHN 15:4 AND PERSONALIZE IT BY REPLACING ANY "YOU", "YOUR" TYPE WORDS WITH "I", "ME", AND "MY".

We can choose to not act on our thoughts

DAY 4: CHOOSE WHAT YOU WEAR

Have you ever dramatically changed your hair style or hair color?

I have. I admit it. I love to experiment with different hair colors. A few months ago, I decided to change my hair color to a very dark reddish brown. I called it my cherry chocolate hair. At first, I was totally in love with my new hair color. It was spunky and made me feel great.

However, after a few weeks, when my lighter natural color started showing at the roots, all I could see was my scary pale white scalp—so much of it that I thought I was losing my hair! After another trip to the hair salon, and over four hours to strip all that dark color away, I had something very close to my natural color back.

As we learn to change our thought patterns, we might experience both extremes—like I did with my cherry chocolate hair color. We get excited and hopeful because we don't have to think like we did before. Yet, the grind of practicing a new way of thinking sinks in. We feel insecure. We start to doubt.

The good news is that we have a choice daily. We can choose to keep our old way of thinking, or we can choose to practice our new way of thinking.

A NEW OUTFIT

FILL IN THE MISSING WORDS FROM EPHESIANS 4:22-24 (NIV):

> You were taught, with regard to your former way of life, to
>
> _____ _____ your old self, which is being
>
> corrupted by its deceitful desires; to be made new in the
>
> attitude of your minds; and to _____ _____ the
>
> new self, created to be like God in true righteousness and
>
> holiness.

Just like we change clothes every day, we must take off (or "put off") our old ways of thinking and change into (or "put on") our new ways of thinking.

The Moody Bible Commentary says this about Ephesians 4:22-24 [emphasis mine]:

> *Though followers of Christ are already made new, they are commanded to put on the new self. That is, they must apply his teaching to their lives... Conversely, **if the new self is put on, the old corrupted self must be laid aside**.*[1]

---

[1] Rydelnik, Michael, et al. "Ephesians 4:22-24". *The Moody Bible Commentary*. Chicago: Moody Press, 2014. Accessed 26 May 2018. Olive Tree Bible Software.

When we want to change our thought patterns, we must replace our negative thoughts (old corrupt self) with positive thoughts based on the principles we find in Scripture (new self). The rest of this study will help you learn and practice this.

ACCORDING TO THE QUOTE ABOVE, HOW DO WE PUT ON OUR NEW SELF?

HOW CAN WE APPLY JESUS' TEACHING TO OUR LIVES?

So, what outfit will you choose to wear? The old self that is corrupt or the new self that is righteous and holy?

IS THERE A THOUGHT PATTERN YOU NEED TO PUT OFF?

WHAT NEW THOUGHT PATTERN WILL HELP YOU TO REPLACE THE OLD THOUGHT PATTERN?

WRITE A BRIEF PRAYER TO THE SPIRIT ABOUT WHAT YOU WANT TO CHOOSE TO WEAR AND ASK FOR HIS HELP.

PERSONALIZE EPHESIANS 4:22-24 BELOW BY REPLACING ANY "YOU", "YOUR" TYPE WORDS WITH "I", "ME", AND "MY".

DAY 5: EMBRACE CHANGE

As we learn to be transformed, we need to embrace change and invest in our healing. I know what you're thinking. Even though this *sounds* good, how do I change how I think?

1. Commit to the Lord
2. Trust His Word
3. Think about it
4. Guard your heart

STEP 1: COMMIT TO THE LORD

The first step is to commit the process of changing our thought patterns to the Lord.

Proverbs 16:3 (NLT) says, "Commit your actions to the Lord, and your plans will succeed."

The NIV says, "Commit your way to the Lord, and he will establish your plans."

The HCSB says, "Commit your activities to the Lord, and your plans will be achieved."

TAKE A FEW MINUTES TO WRITE A PRAYER TO GOD COMMITTING TO CHANGE YOUR THINKING.

STEP 2: TRUST HIS WORD

Let's take a few minutes to look at how the Bible can help us in our transformation process.

WHAT DOES HEBREWS 4:12 SAY ABOUT THE WORD OF GOD?

WHAT DOES 2 TIMOTHY 3:16-17 SAY ABOUT SCRIPTURE?

ACCORDING TO 2 TIMOTHY 3:17, WHAT IS THE PURPOSE OF SCRIPTURE?

Scripture judges our thoughts and our hearts (attitudes). It can teach us what we need to learn, and it equips us for life.

WHAT PURPOSE DO BIBLE STORIES SERVE (SEE 1 CORINTHIANS 10:6)?

Not only does Scripture instruct us and give us direction, it also provides us with many examples of real people who walked the earth and it highlights the good and bad things they did. We also have the parables of Jesus that help us understand how to live and think.

STEP 3: THINK ABOUT IT

To change our thinking, we first must know what we are thinking about. We must understand where we are to get to where we want to go. The good news is that we can think about what we are thinking about. One way to do this is to meditate on and evaluate our thoughts.

One valuable way to evaluate our thoughts is to write them down. I am a huge advocate of journaling the journey.

There are many benefits of journaling:

1. It gives us a way to work through what is currently on our mind.
2. It also provides a record of our growth.
3. We can clearly see God's hand in our lives.
4. It bolsters us in our current circumstances by helping us remember what we have already overcome.
5. It is a great way to keep verses, quotes, etc. handy for those times of crisis.

STEP 4: GUARD YOUR HEART

We do not have to accept every thought that comes into our minds. We can evaluate where the thought comes from and if it is worthy of our attention. This is what it means to guard our hearts.

READ PROVERBS 4:23. WHAT ARE SOME STEPS YOU CAN TAKE TO GUARD YOUR HEART?

We are not slaves to every thought that pops into our heart

Practical Ways to Guard Your Heart:

1. Evaluate your thoughts and what is on your heart.
2. Root out thoughts that you should let go of, including:
   a. Self-condemning thoughts
   b. Berating thoughts
   c. Judging thoughts
   d. Bitterness
   e. Envy
   f. Any negative thought
3. Store up good thoughts about yourself and others.

ACCORDING TO GALATIANS 5:16, HOW DO YOU KEEP FROM GRATIFYING THE DESIRES OF THE FLESH?

WHAT DOES THAT MEAN?

"Walking by the Spirit" means that we look to the Spirit for guidance. It's a lifestyle.

PICK A VERSE FROM TODAY'S LESSON AND PERSONALIZE IT.

Then we will no longer be infants, tossed back and forth by the waves, and blown here and there by every wind of teaching and by the cunning and craftiness of people in their deceitful scheming.

–Ephesians 4:14

EXPECT TRIALS

We should _____ to face _____ and

difficult _____ in life. (John 16:33)

DEALING WITH TRIALS

A _____ foundation is _____.

A foundation built on _____ _____
under pressure. (Matt. 7:27)

_____ is the _____ of God, the influence of

the _____, and the _____ of Christ.

A foundation built on _____ _____ under
pressure. (Matt. 7:25)

BUILDING ON THE ROCK

GOD'S WORD

When we _____ our Bibles we learn about _____,

_____ and how to _____ our lives.

INFLUENCE OF THE SPIRIT

The Spirit is our _____ and he _____
us of what Jesus said. (John 14:26)

The Spirit _____ us in our _____.
(Romans 8:26)

The Spirit _____ for us when we don't know

what to _____. (Romans 8:26-27)

TRUTH OF CHRIST

When we _____ the _____ of Christ

and our _____ in Him, we build a strong foundation.

(John 14:6)

_____

_____

_____

_____

_____

_____

_____

_____

_____

_____

_____

_____

_____

_____

_____

_____

_____

A person may think their own ways are right, but the Lord weighs the heart. —Proverbs 21:2

When I was a child, I believed in Santa Claus. Each Christmas morning that I woke to find presents under the tree only reinforced my belief in Santa. I mean, how else did all those presents get there?

Then came the sad day when my parents told me the truth. Santa Claus was fiction. I was crushed, and I no longer believed.

The same thing can happen with other beliefs. To us, something can be irrefutably true. We can be one-hundred percent convinced that something is real, even though it is not the truth.

What happens when we discover that we believed a lie? We can become depressed, angry, bitter, resentful, and a whole host of other feelings.

The lies we tell ourselves seem completely real to us

The same idea is true concerning our thoughts. For years I believed that I was worthless. It caused me to act a certain way and to talk a certain way. What I believed to be true in my mind was really a lie— especially in light of God's Word—but it seemed completely real to me at the time.

This week we'll focus on some of the lies that we tell ourselves and refute those lies with truth from scripture.

Remember to highlight or mark anything that speaks to you, especially verses so we can use them during the last week.

DAY 1: I'M NOT _____ ENOUGH

I'm not good enough. I'm not pretty enough. I'm not smart enough. I'm not loved enough.

No matter what lie we listen to, the "I'm not (good, smart, pretty, loved) enough" mindset keeps us feeling less than others.

These thoughts and feelings are born out of past experiences where we compared ourselves to others and believed we came up lacking. Or perhaps there was someone in your life in a position of authority, like a parent or teacher, who wrongfully said these things to you. Maybe you were like me as a child and didn't always fit in. These feelings could have come from classmates picking on you. Perhaps you suffered abuse that left you believing something about yourself that was not true.

Regardless of where these feelings and thoughts originated, there is a good chance we are holding on to them as if they are truth when they are not.

More about that in a minute. First, I want to look at what the Bible says about comparing ourselves to others.

WHAT DOES GALATIANS 6:3-5 SAY ABOUT COMPARING OURSELVES TO OTHERS?

IN VERSE 4, IT SAYS, "EACH ONE SHOULD TEST THEIR OWN ACTIONS." WHAT DO YOU THINK THIS MEANS?

When we compare ourselves to others and tell ourselves that we come up short, we are carrying a heavy load that we were never meant to carry. The only person you need to worry about is you and you are an amazing person—the person God created you to be.

Some characteristics of a person who feels "less than" include:

1. Always apologizes for things that you have no control over. "I'm sorry I spilled my coffee." "Sorry dinner is late." We don't have to be sorry for normal life. Sometimes dinner will just be late. Sometimes we'll be klutzy and spill things. That doesn't mean we owe someone an apology.

2. Makes excuses for everything. "I was caught behind a slow customer." "There was too much traffic." "My mom called and…" We feel the need to blame circumstances for something we feel should have turned out differently.

3. Explains herself far too often. "I had to stop on the way home." "I was just double checking the report before I send it out." None of these things are bad things, yet we feel the need to constantly justify and explain our actions.

4. <u>Defensive. Friends say she takes things too personally.</u> "I didn't do that." "That wasn't my intention." This one is still a sore spot for me. I have been told most of my life that I take things too personally. Until recently, I didn't understand that when something bad happened it was not my fault.

CAN YOU IDENTIFY WITH ONE OR MORE OF THE CHARACTERISTICS ABOVE? TAKE A MINUTE TO WRITE ABOUT IT.

SMART ENOUGH

Intelligence or smarts can really be boiled down to wisdom. Wisdom is the type of smarts that really matters the most. Think about it. Who do you respect more, someone who can quote the elements from the periodic table or someone who understands how to navigate difficult circumstances?

READ JAMES 3:13-18. WHERE DOES TRUE WISDOM COME FROM?

WHAT ARE THE CHARACTERISTICS OF THE WISE AND UNDERSTANDING (V13)?

WHAT ARE THE CHARACTERISTICS OF WORLDLY WISDOM? WHAT IS THE
ENVIRONMENT THAT COMES FROM FOLLOWING WORLDLY WISDOM?

WHAT ARE THE CHARACTERISTICS OF HEAVENLY WISDOM (V17)?

We can choose to pursue worldly wisdom or heavenly wisdom.
When we pursue a good life of humility, we are seeking heavenly
wisdom.

One more note for those of us who might be hung up on not being
intelligent enough. James 1:5 says that if we lack wisdom (or
intelligence), we should ask God and it will be given to us.

BEAUTIFUL ENOUGH

You are beautiful. Take a second. Say those words out loud. "I am
beautiful."

Not feeling it? That's okay. Keep saying it out loud. If you tell yourself
something enough times, you will eventually believe it.

God's Word is clear that He defines beauty differently than the world
does. Read the following verses and make note of what beauty is to
God.

1 PETER 3:3-4

1 SAMUEL 16:7

Wow! Our spirit, our inner self, is where our true beauty comes from. Why do we spend so much time handing over our self-worth to the world and its opinion when God's is the only one that matters?

If you're still not convinced, then look at what Galatians 3:26-27 says:

> So in Christ Jesus you are all children of God through faith, for all of you who were baptized into Christ have clothed yourselves with Christ.

Christ gave us the most beautiful sacrifice and we are clothed with him. When God looks at us, he sees Christ.

GOOD ENOUGH

READ 1 PETER 2:9. WHAT ARE WE CALLED?

I think anyone who is a "royal priesthood" and "chosen people" is good enough.

LOVED ENOUGH

Romans 8:39 says that nothing can separate us from God's love. There is no love that is greater than His. If you believe in Him, you are deeply and incredibly loved.

WHAT DOES PSALM 36:5-7 SAY ABOUT GOD'S LOVE?

God's love is unfailing, and His love matters the most. He loves you deeply and, in the way that no human ever could. When you start to feel unloved, remember the verses we studied today.

God's opinion of us is the only one that matters

PERSONALIZE IT

FILL IN THE BLANK:

I'm not _____ enough.

WHERE DID THIS BELIEF COME FROM?

ASK THE SPIRIT TO BEGIN SHOWING YOU THE TRUTH ABOUT YOUR IDENTITY. WRITE DOWN WHAT HE IS SAYING TO YOU.

PICK ONE VERSE FROM TODAY'S LESSON AND PERSONALIZE IT BELOW.

DAY 2: PUT DOWN YOUR BAT

Have you ever walked away from a conversation at work or home and later played back the conversation repeatedly in your head? I have. Many times.

On one such occasion, I replayed the conversation in my head for days. After the replay, I would start telling myself all kinds of horrible things like:

> *I'm such an idiot. How could I have said that? I don't know why I always let my emotions get to me. What a stupid, stupid thing to do. I'm such an idiot.*

Some of us would call that beating ourselves up. If there was a professional league for such a thing, I would be on the all pro team. That's how good I am at beating myself up.

PERSONAL REFLECTION: THINK ABOUT A TIME WHEN YOU REPLAYED A CONVERSATION IN YOUR HEAD. WHAT KINDS OF THINGS DID YOU SAY TO YOURSELF? HOW DID THAT MAKE YOU FEEL? WAS YOUR SELF-TALK HELPFUL OR HARMFUL?

The problem with beating up ourselves is that it seeps deep into our souls. We start to believe the things we say and that we deserve condemnation.

CONDEMNATION

This type of thinking is called self-condemnation. What is self-condemnation? Several online dictionaries define it as *an admission you have failed to do or be something you know you should do or be.*[2]

That definition seems too much like self-evaluation and does not clearly express the depth of pain associated with real-life self-condemnation. I would define self-condemnation as a hypercritical negative awareness of one's failures and short-comings to the point of losing the ability to objectively see one's positive attributes.

---

[2] "SELF-CONDEMNATION." *What Does Self-condemnation Mean? Definition, Meaning and Pronunciation* (Free English Language Dictionary). N.p., n.d. Web. 03 Mar. 2016.

This type of thinking is not what God desires of us.

READ ROMANS 8:1-2. WHAT DOES IT SAY ABOUT CONDEMNATION?

That's right. When we are in Jesus, we are no longer condemned. Not by God. Not by His Word. So why do we persist in condemning ourselves?

If you were to look up antonyms for the word condemnation, you might find some of these words:

Approval	Sanction	Pardon
Praise	Absolution	Release
Compliment	Acquittal	Freeing
Endorsement	Exoneration	

TAKE A MINUTE TO REFLECT ON THESE WORDS. CIRCLE THE ONES THAT MEAN THE MOST TO YOU. WHY DO THESE MEAN SO MUCH TO YOU?

FILL IN THE BLANKS BELOW FROM JOHN 3:17 NIV.

For God did not send his Son into the world to

_____ the world, but to _____ the

world through him.

READ 2 CORINTHIANS 5:21. WHAT DID JESUS DO? BECAUSE OF WHAT JESUS DID, HOW DOES GOD SEE US?

WHAT DOES PSALM 34:22 SAY ABOUT CONDEMNATION?

God's Word says there is no more condemnation or judgment or blame for those of us in Christ Jesus. We have His pardon, endorsement, absolution, and approval.

WHAT KEEPS YOU FROM BELIEVING THIS?

FORGIVENESS

Forgiveness is a word that sums up the opposite of condemnation. The Bible talks about the forgiveness God gives us and the forgiveness we give others. If you have ever had reason to forgive someone for horrible wrongs, you've probably experienced a tremendous feeling of freedom when you forgave them.

WHAT DO THE FOLLOWING VERSES SAY ABOUT FORGIVENESS?

PSALM 103:11-12

ISAIAH 43:25

God does not remember our sins so the next time you find yourself replaying a conversation and recounting your failures, remember that God forgives and forgets our sins.

Put down your bat, stop beating yourself up, and learn to forgive yourself.

IS THERE SOMETHING YOU NEED TO FORGIVE YOURSELF FOR? TAKE SOME TIME TO JOURNAL AND PRAY ABOUT IT.

PICK ONE VERSE FROM TODAY'S LESSON AND PERSONALIZE IT BELOW.

DAY 3: SHUCK THE SHOULDS

After a long day at work followed by sitting in traffic, I often have the thought that I "should" make dinner. Sometimes, I don't feel like it. Though more often than not, I drum up the will power to cook dinner.

Maybe you find yourself often thinking about what you should or should not do. I should go to the store. I should put on makeup today. I should be kinder to my husband. I should be patient with my kids when I discipline them.

REFLECT ON THE LAST TIME YOU TOLD YOURSELF YOU "SHOULD" DO SOMETHING OR ACT A PARTICULAR WAY. WRITE DOWN SOME NOTES ABOUT IT.

HOW OFTEN DO YOU TELL YOURSELF YOU "SHOULD" DO SOMETHING OR BE SOMETHING?

WHY DO YOU SAY THESE THINGS TO YOURSELF?

Let's see where these "shoulds" come from.

MY EXPECTATIONS

Sometimes those "shoulds" come from expectations we have of ourselves or from expectations that others have of us. They may even be expectations from our past.

Those of us who are Type A people tend to be driven by self-imposed expectations. With a tendency towards perfectionism, we expect everything we do to be perfect.

Rarely, does life turn out perfectly. And when us Type A's hit those road bumps, we turn critical accusations toward ourselves.

For all of us who have high—dare I say, unrealistic—expectations of ourselves, we need to let go of the heavy burden of our own expectations.

READ MATTHEW 11:28-30. WHAT DOES JESUS SAY HE WILL GIVE US?

WHAT IS JESUS' WAY ACCORDING TO THESE VERSES?

Through imperfect progress, we become like Jesus

If we follow the way that Jesus modeled for us and we learn from him, we can find deep soul-rest. His way happens through imperfect progress and not perfection.

WHERE DO YOU HAVE UNREALISTIC EXPECTATIONS OF YOURSELF RIGHT NOW?

WHAT CAN YOU TELL YOURSELF TO KEEP YOUR EXPECTATIONS IN CHECK?

OTHERS' EXPECTATIONS

Some of the "shoulds" we say to ourselves come from growing up with demanding or controlling influencers in our lives. Perhaps a parent or teacher or coach had very high expectations of us. Or perhaps we lived with a critical parent whose expectations could never be met.

In the cases where we developed a pattern of thinking based on other people's expectations, we need to remember that God's opinion is the only one that matters. If we are meeting His expectations of us and living under His grace and mercy, we do not need to give a millisecond's thought to the expectations of others.

WHAT DO THE FOLLOWING VERSES SAY ABOUT PLEASING OTHERS?

PROVERBS 29:25

ISAIAH 2:22

ISAIAH 51:7

GALATIANS 1:10

In the end, we need to be careful how much weight we put on what others say or think about us.

IN WHAT WAYS DO YOU PLACE TOO MUCH EMPHASIS ON OTHER PEOPLE'S EXPECTATIONS?

WHAT CAN YOU DO DIFFERENTLY TO CHANGE YOUR THINKING IN THIS AREA?

TIP: Consider memorizing this verse or placing it somewhere you will see it often to remind you to change your thinking.

DAY 4: BLAME GAME

Do you blame others? Do you blame your circumstances? Are you always making excuses?

I had no idea I had a blaming problem until I started thinking about what I said and what thoughts prompted my speech. I would say things like:

"I'm sorry I'm late. Traffic was really bad."

"I don't think I could do that. No one ever taught me how."

"It's not my fault."

"The devil made me do it."

When I really spent time thinking about why I would say such things, I began to realize that most of the time I was afraid of what others would think of me or that I would not measure up.

BLAME DISGUISES TRUTH

Regardless of why I was blaming others or my circumstances, I was hiding something I perceived to be wrong.

I was late to work when I knew it was important to be on time, so I made an excuse. The truth was that I did not leave early enough to allow me to arrive on time.

I felt insecure when someone asked me to do something that I didn't know how to do, but I thought they expected me to already know, so I made an excuse. The truth was that I made an assumption about the other person's expectations and I allowed myself to give into fear and insecurity.

Let's study an example of blame from the Bible.

READ GENESIS 3:1-19. WHAT DID ADAM AND EVE DO TO DISGUISE THE TRUTH?

WHO DID EVE BLAME (V13) AND WHO DID ADAM BLAME (V12)?

Pay close attention to verse 12. Adam directly blamed Eve, but indirectly blamed God when he said, "the woman you put here with me."

When we blame others, we are lying to someone else, to God, or to ourselves.

WHAT WERE THE CONSEQUENCES OF ADAM AND EVE'S CHOICE (V16-19)?

Even before the sin was committed, Eve tried to rationalize the action she wanted to take. In verse 6, she listened to the serpent and saw that the fruit looked delicious. Rationalization and justification are warning signs that we are about to get ourselves into a bad situation that will likely lead us to blame someone.

OWN YOUR STUFF

One way to change from a blame and excuse driven mindset is to take ownership of your stuff.

WHO APPEARS BEFORE THE JUDGMENT SEAT ACCORDING TO ROMANS 14:12 AND 2 CORINTHIANS 5:10?

Because we are accountable for the things we say and do, whether good or bad, it does not make sense for us to blame others or even Satan for the things that come out of our mouths. We must take ownership of our words and actions if we truly desire to change.

Macmillan online dictionary defines ownership as:

> An attitude of accepting responsibility for something and taking control of how it develops.[3]

WHAT PART OF THIS DEFINITION STANDS OUT THE MOST TO YOU?

PERSONAL REFLECTION: DO YOU BELIEVE THAT YOU CAN TAKE CONTROL OF YOUR THOUGHTS AND HOW THEY DEVELOP? WHY OR WHY NOT?

In 2 Peter 1:5-7 it says:

> For this very reason, _make every effort_ to add to your faith goodness; and to goodness, knowledge; and to knowledge, self-control; and to self-control, perseverance; and to perseverance, godliness; and to godliness, mutual affection; and to mutual affection, love.

---

[3] "Ownership American English Definition and Synonyms | Macmillan Dictionary." _Ownership American English Definition and Synonyms_ | Macmillan Dictionary. N.p., n.d. Web. 03 Apr. 2016.

The phrase "make every effort" implies that we can affect change in our lives, especially in these areas.

Circle the word "self-control" in the above verses.

You have the capability to take ownership for your words, thoughts, and emotions. You can become self-controlled in these areas.

How? By studying, practicing, and praying about your thoughts. This is not a one-time deal. It's a lifelong effort.

PICK A VERSE FROM TODAY'S LESSON AND PERSONALIZE IT.

DAY 5: DOWNWARD SPIRAL

Despair. It's a very dark and lonely place to be and I have been there.

In late 2012, I was dealing with some severe back pain. I had many different treatments to try to help, only nothing seemed to work long-term. Then in early December, I got a sinus infection. I felt horrible.

One night as I lay on the couch in the living room, to keep from waking up my husband, I suffered a terrible coughing fit. The pain in my back went from horrible to even worse. The next morning, I could barely walk and started losing some of the feeling in my right leg.

Over the next few weeks, I tried more treatments. I slipped into despair and wondered if I would ever feel normal again.

I eventually had back surgery and after the recovery period, began to feel well for several years.

Although, in that darkest time, anything that went wrong in life only added to my despair. If someone cut me off in traffic or I got into an argument with my husband or co-worker, I sank deeper and deeper.

CALL ON HIM

One of the things I learned through looking back on that season of my life is that I could have called on God more than I had.

The story of David from 1 Samuel 30:1-8 shows us how we can choose to react in the face of despair and distress.

WHAT DOES 1 SAMUEL 30:2-3 SAY HAPPENED TO DAVID'S AND HIS MEN'S FAMILIES?

WHAT WERE THE MEN'S REACTIONS IN VERSE 4?

WHAT DID DAVID DO AT THE END OF VERSE 6 AND IN VERSE 7?

The ephod referenced in verse 7 was a sacred garment worn by the high priest and often used as an oracle or means of seeking God's direction. [4] It was unusual for someone other than a priest to wear it. David was an exception and had used it before to understand God's will. [5]

---

[4] Nave, Orville J. "Entry for 'Ephod'". Naves Topical Bible Index. 1896. Accessed 3 April 2016. Olive Tree Bible Software.

[5] Rydelnik, Michael, et al. "2 Samuel 30:7-8". *The Moody Bible Commentary*. Chicago: Moody Press, 2014. Accessed 3 April 2014. Olive Tree Bible Software.

READ PSALM 18:6. WHAT FURTHER INSIGHT DO WE GET ABOUT DAVID'S ACTIONS FROM THIS VERSE?

In a time of despair and distress, David's men moved from despair to anger and then they blamed David for the trouble. Verse 6 says that they were "bitter in spirit".

If we're not careful our despair and distress can turn to bitterness, anger, and blame.

Or we can choose to react like David did by turning to God for strength.

DESPAIR TO PRAISE

In a time of despair when we feel like we cannot see anything except the bad around us, it is helpful to shift our thinking by focusing on God instead.

There are many ways we can do this. The Psalms are a wonderful place to start. Read them or say them aloud. Singing worship songs can also help. We don't have to be in the mood to sing. If we try, we might find our mood improved by the end of a song or two.

WHAT DO THE FOLLOWING VERSES SAY ABOUT DESPAIR, DISTRESS, OR TRIALS?

2 SAMUEL 24:14

PSALM 55:16-18

ISAIAH 61:3

We can have our despair replaced with joy when we turn our thoughts towards God. We can get a change of perspective, like the apostle Paul talked about in 2 Corinthians 4:8-9. He acknowledged that he was facing some hard times, but he also acknowledged that he was not abandoned or crushed or destroyed.

When we feel crushed or abandoned or destroyed, if we look to our source of strength, He will provide for us.

PERSONAL REFLECTION: ARE THERE SOME VERSES YOU'VE READ OR HIGHLIGHTED IN YOUR BIBLE THAT WOULD HELP YOU THE NEXT TIME YOU FEEL DESPAIR? IF SO, JOT THEM DOWN HERE. IF NOT, TAKE A LOOK AT PSALM 77 OR PSALM 34 AND WRITE DOWN THE VERSES THAT SPEAK TO YOU.

PICK A VERSE FROM TODAY AND PERSONALIZE IT BELOW.

Let your eyes look straight ahead; fix your gaze directly before you. Give careful thought to the paths for your feet and be steadfast in all your ways. Do not turn to the right or the left; keep your foot from evil. –Proverbs 4:25-27

The two enemies of our minds: _____ _____

and _____.

THE FLESH

WHAT IS IT? (GALATIANS 5:13-26)

In contexts like this, the Greek word for flesh (sarx) refers to the sinful state of human beings, often presented as a power in opposition to the Spirit. –NIV footnote

- The NIV uses the phrase, "_____ _____".

- NLT uses "_____ _____"

- NASB uses "_____ _____"

- CEB uses "selfish _____" or "selfish

   _____"

FIGHTING THE FLESH

_____ by the _____ keeps us from

falling _____ to our _____. (Gal. 5:16)

SATAN

Satan's plan is to steal our _____, kill our _____,

and destroy our _____ with _____.

(John 10:10)

SATAN'S NAMES AND TACTICS

Tactic 1: Satan uses our _____ to

_____, _____, or _____

us from God's plan. (Job 1:6-12)

Tactic 2: The Devil _____ _____

to _____ us away from God. (Matt. 4:1-11)

Tactic 3: The Tempter _____ us in order to _____

us away from our _____. (Matt. 4:3, 1 Thess. 3:4-5)

Tactic 4: The father of _____ _____ us to

believe _____ instead of the truth. (John 8:44)

OUR WEAPONS

Weapon 1: Proactive prayer _____ our hearts on

_____ and His _____. (John 17:15)

Weapon 2: The _____ is found in _____.

To _____ it, we must _____ it. (Matt. 4:1-11)

Weapon 3: _____ _____ to Jesus's teachings in order to

know the _____. (John 8:31-32)

More Weapons: Armor of God. (Ephesians 6)

_____

_____

_____

In Session 3, we talked about our enemies: the flesh and Satan. However, I want to clear up a few misconceptions about our enemy, Satan.

As we learn to change our thoughts, it is important to understand some of the characteristics of Satan and the **limits** of his power.

Moody's Bible Commentary states that Ezekiel 28:11-19 is the record of the downfall of Satan[6] (who was the power behind the King of Tyre mentioned in verse 12).

LIST EVERYTHING YOU LEARN ABOUT SATAN FROM EZEKIEL 28:11-19.

From the Ezekiel passage, we see that Satan:

- Is beautiful (v13)
- Was in the garden of Eden (v13)
- Is a created being (v15)
- Is prideful (v17, 1 Timothy 3:6) and wicked (v15)
- Expelled from the mountain of God / heaven (v14, 16, 19)
- Still has access to God (v13, Job 1:6-12, Zechariah 3:1-2)
- His days are numbered (v19)

Many times, we think of Satan as equal with God. But, he is not. He is a created being and is restricted by the same things that restrict other created beings like angels.

Satan cannot be everywhere at one time (omnipresent). He comes and goes according to Matthew 4:3, 11 and Job 1:7-12.

There are two theories, according to J. I. Packer, about how Satan influences so many people. One is that he is multi-present, like

---

[6] Rydelnik, Michael, et al. "Ezekiel 28:11-19". *The Moody Bible Commentary*. Chicago: Moody Press, 2014. Accessed 9 April 2016. Olive Tree Bible Software.

angels, meaning he has limits though not quite as many as humans. The second is that he is the leader and he sends out his demons to influence us.[7]

Satan cannot know our thoughts (omniscient). Nevertheless, he can observe our reactions and interactions. He has had many millennia to study human nature, so it may feel like he knows our thoughts. Think of it like when you guess what someone might be thinking based on their behavior.

Only God is omnipresent (Psalm 139, John 1) and omniscient (1 Kings 8:39). God alone knows our thoughts and Jesus, as incarnate of God, has the same characteristic (John 2:25, Matthew 9:4, John 6:64).

FROM THE SCRIPTURES PRESENTED IN SESSION 3 AND IN THIS DEEPER DIVE, WHAT DID YOU LEARN ABOUT SATAN?

WHY DO YOU THINK IT IS IMPORTANT TO UNDERSTAND WHO SATAN IS AND WHAT HE CAN DO?

---

[7] Packer, J.I. "Is Satan Omnipresent?" *Christianity Today.* Christianity Today Mag., 19 Sept 2000. Web. Accessed 9 April 2016. <http://www.christianitytoday.com/ct/2000/september4/36.115.html >

I do not understand what I do. For what I want to do I do not do, but what I hate I do. –Romans 7:15

As we start Week 3, it is important to remember that changing our thinking is a process. We will have both good days, where we do what we intend to do, and we will have bad days, where we do not do what we intend to do.

Any time we try to change ourselves, we are bound to run into a few stumbling blocks. This week we will learn about five that can slow our progress as we change our thought patterns.

DAY 1: IDENTITY CRISIS

This stumbling block hits close to home for me. So many times in my life I have tried to get my identity from my career, my achievements, my spouse, or my success.

My identity was wrapped up in what I did. If I was successful at work, then I was good. If there was a crisis at work, then my world was shaken.

IF YOU ARE REALLY HONEST WITH YOURSELF, WHERE WOULD YOU SAY YOU GET YOUR IDENTITY? IS IT FROM BEING A MOM OR A WIFE? IS IT FROM HOW MUCH MONEY IS IN YOUR BANK ACCOUNT? IS IT FROM YOUR JOB?

According to Priscilla Shirer, the word "saved" means more than just being saved from death. We are also saved into health, wholeness, and victory.[8]

The key to experiencing a healthy mind, a whole heart, and victory over our thoughts requires that we actually use our salvation.

Our true identity rests in who God says we are

What does this look like on a day to day basis? First, we learn about and actively remember that our identity is in Christ. We are called children of God, precious in His sight, chosen and dearly loved. The list from Scripture goes on and on. Our job is to learn about our identity until it fills our minds and hearts and pushes out any negative thoughts that come from our flesh or Satan.

Our true identity is not based on what we have or what we can do. It rests solely in who God says we are.

READ EPHESIANS 1:3-6. HOW DOES GOD SEE US ACCORDING TO VERSE 4?

WHAT DID GOD PREDESTINE US FOR (V5)?

WHAT DOES ROMANS 8:15-16 SAY ABOUT US? HOW IS THIS SIMILAR TO EPHESIANS 1:5?

WHAT DOES JOHN 1:12-13 SAY ABOUT THOSE WHO BELIEVE IN HIS NAME?

---

[8] Shirer, Priscilla. "Session 6: Helmet of Salvation." *Armor of God.* LifeWay Christian Resources, 07 Aug. 2015. Web. 26 Apr. 2016.

We are the adopted children of God, through Jesus. Ephesians 1:4-5 says that our adoption comes from God's love and it lines up with his pleasure and will. God wants you. He loves you. He calls you his own child. And He takes pleasure in you.

IN HIS IMAGE

We are a culture obsessed with image. We post pictures of our families on social media. We spend hours getting ready in the morning, all so we can put forward an image to others—hoping they will see only what we want them to see.

Yet, amid all this image-making, sometimes we forget who our real image takes after.

READ GENESIS 1:26-27. WHO WAS CREATED IN GOD'S IMAGE OR LIKENESS?

That's right; you were made in God's likeness and on purpose.

READ 1 JOHN 3:2. WHAT ARE WE TO GOD? WHO WILL WE BE LIKE?

INTIMATE KNOWLEDGE

Much of my younger years growing up, despite my parents' best efforts, I struggled to believe that anyone loved me or truly knew me. I am guarded and even though I share openly with friends in a

Bible study, I sometimes tend to hold back the inner most parts of myself.

Regardless, there is One who knows me better than any other. When I remember just how well He knows me, it helps shift my perspective from what I think I lack to what I have in Him.

READ THE FOLLOWING PASSAGE FROM THE MESSAGE.

> *Oh yes, you shaped me first inside, then out;*
>
> > *you formed me in my mother's womb.*
>
> *I thank you, High God—you're breathtaking!*
>
> > *Body and soul, I am marvelously made!*
> >
> > *I worship in adoration—what a creation!*
>
> *You know me inside and out,*
>
> > *you know every bone in my body;*
>
> *You know exactly how I was made, bit by bit,*
>
> > *how I was sculpted from nothing into something.*
>
> *Like an open book, you watched me grow from conception to birth;*
>
> > *all the stages of my life were spread out before you,*
>
> *The days of my life all prepared*
>
> > *before I'd even lived one day.*
>
> > > *—Psalm 139:13-16 (The Message)*

LIST EVERYTHING THAT GOD DOES ACCORDING TO PSALM 139:13-16 (ABOVE).

God loves you and knows you so intimately—right down to the hairs on your head. He even knows your natural hair color! He also knows the things you love about yourself and the things you hate about yourself.

WHAT ENCOURAGEMENT CAN YOU FIND FOR THE THINGS YOU DON'T LIKE ABOUT YOURSELF WHEN YOU READ 2 CORINTHIANS 12:9?

TAKE A MINUTE TO WRITE DOWN TWO THINGS YOU'VE LEARNED ABOUT YOUR IDENTITY FROM TODAY'S LESSON.

1. _____

2. _____

TIP: Consider transferring these to a notecard that you will see through-out your day to remind you of your true identity.

PICK ONE VERSE FROM TODAY AND PERSONALIZE IT BELOW.

DAY 2: PERFECTIONISM'S UGLY SIDE

I'm a recovering perfectionist and overachiever. I don't really know where these traits first manifested themselves, but they have always been a part of my life.

I applied perfectionism to every part of my life. I wanted to look perfect and act perfect and be perfect at work, at home, and with my friends. I invested a great deal of energy anticipating the needs of my husband, friends, family, and coworkers.

I also had plans A-Z for everything. Then I discovered that the planning part of perfectionism was considered an asset in business. I came up with great plans for building software and for keeping my team on track.

Until one day it all came crashing down around me.

The important project I was on became a heavy burden. The client was never satisfied with the extra effort I put in. No matter what I did, they wanted more. So, I gave them more. I worked eighty hours a week for a period, sacrificing time with my husband, just to try to perfectly meet their unrealistic expectations.

Then I developed health problems. The late nights and early mornings had caught up with me. My stomach hurt all the time. I was emotionally, mentally, and physically drained.

PERSONAL REFLECTION: CAN YOU RELATE TO MY STORY? DO YOU STRUGGLE WITH PERFECTIONIST TENDENCIES? IF SO, HOW DOES THIS AFFECT THE WAY YOU FEEL ABOUT YOURSELF? ABOUT OTHERS?

Perfectionism kills us from the inside out

When I look back on that time in my life, I can sum it up best with this thought: Perfectionism is the idolatry of an unachievable standard that leaves us with the illusion that we are good. Perfectionism kills us from the inside out.

WHAT DOES PROVERBS 16:9 AND PROVERBS 19:21 SAY ABOUT OUR PLANS AND GOD'S PLANS?

HOW CAN WE APPLY THESE VERSES TO OUR THOUGHTS WHEN WE ARE STRIVING FOR PERFECTION?

READ 2 CORINTHIANS 12:9. WHAT IS OUR STATE WHEN GOD'S POWER IS MADE PERFECT?

WHAT DOES GOD PROVIDE TO SUSTAIN US?

LEGALISM

For the Christian, sometimes perfectionism is rooted in legalism. When we follow all the rules, we assume our life will be perfect. Yet it is not. Nor can it ever be. Not while we live on earth.

Merriam-Webster defines legalism as: "strict, literal, or excessive conformity to the law or to a religious or moral code."[9]

If we are not careful, we can turn our faith into a set of rules to be followed. When we do this, we miss the meaning of the principles set forth in Scripture. We dumb down those principles into "dos" and "don'ts" instead of meditating on and applying the meaning of those principles to our lives.

READ MATTHEW 23:23-28. WHAT DOES JESUS CALL THE PHARISEES (V. 23, 25, 27)?

---

[9] "legalism." *Merriam-Webster.com*. Merriam-Webster, 2011. Web. 17 Apr 2016.

WHAT DID THEY NEGLECT ACCORDING TO VERSE 23? WHAT DID JESUS SAY THEY SHOULD HAVE PRACTICED IN VERSE 23?

WHAT DID THEY CLEAN ACCORDING TO VERSE 25? WHAT DID JESUS SAY THEY SHOULD CLEAN INSTEAD (V26)?

WHAT HARSH WORDS DID JESUS USE TO REBUKE THE PHARISEES IN VERSES 27 AND 28?

WHAT WAS THE MAIN POINT JESUS WAS TRYING TO MAKE TO THE PHARISEES IN THIS PASSAGE? HOW DOES THIS RELATE TO PERFECTIONISM?

Jesus harshly rebuked the Pharisees in Matthew 23. Some Bibles have a heading for Matthew 23:13-39 that says: "Seven Woes on the Teachers of the Law and the Pharisees."

When we pursue perfectionism in our faith, we are in danger of focusing on the outside of our cup. We can put on a good show and seem pious to those around us. However, on the inside we still harbor the same anger, bitterness, selfishness, greed, or whatever vice or feeling we have struggled with for so long.

Jesus did not come to save us so we could be perfect looking Christians. He came so we could love Him, let Him love us back, and so that His love would flow through us to those without hope around us.

In walking out our faith, our goal should be imperfect progress. We learn a principle and apply it to our lives with the Spirit's help. It is a process that often requires us to take steps forward and backwards to truly learn.

FEAR OF FAILURE

When I was on that project at work, I wanted to look good and feel like I knew what I was doing, so I had a very high standard of how I defined success for myself. Perfectionism was a cover to hide my extreme fear of failure. In fact, perfectionism was a self-fulfilling prophecy of failure. By setting an impossibly high standard for myself, I was guaranteeing my failure.

The two major things I learned from this time were:

1. As Zig Ziglar said, "Failure is an event, not a person."
2. We do not have to fear shame, disgrace, or humiliation if they come because we trust in God.

WHAT DOES ISAIAH 54:4 SAY ABOUT HUMILIATION, DISGRACE, AND SHAME?

READ PSALM 25:1-3. LIST EVERYTHING THESE VERSES SAY ABOUT SHAME.

READ PSALM 34:4-6. HOW DO THESE VERSES DESCRIBE SOMEONE WHOSE FACE IS NEVER COVERED WITH SHAME?

When we seek God, and put our trust in Him, He gives us the power to change our thoughts from those full of fear and shame to thoughts focused on Him. The Psalmist and Isaiah understood that we would still feel shame, disgrace, and humiliation at times. When we focus our eyes on God, we do not have to wallow in these feelings. Our hope is in Him.

PICK ONE VERSE FROM TODAY'S LESSON AND PERSONALIZE IT BELOW.

DAY 3: FALSE GUILT

Have you ever felt guilty for eating a candy bar? Is it a sin to eat a candy bar? What if your blood sugar is low and you need to quickly boost it? Is that a good reason to eat a candy bar?

My answer is yes, to all of the above. There have been times in my life where I felt guilty for eating a candy bar and it was a sin because I was overindulging. There are other times that I have eaten a candy bar because my blood sugar needed a quick boost. That was not a sin and I should not feel bad about that.

There is a big difference between false guilt and conviction. Guilt depresses us and suppresses us. Conviction corrects our behavior and opens us up to forgiveness and reconciliation.

Bruce Narramore and Bill Counts said it this way: "True guilt [conviction] is an **objective fact** but false guilt is a **subjective feeling** of pain and rejection."[10]

False guilt is rooted in feelings, not facts.

False guilt is rooted in feelings, not facts

GUILT

When we feel guilty, how can we know whether it is conviction or false guilt?

Feeling guilty for eating a candy bar or not being a gourmet cook is false guilt. It comes from the feeling that we are not doing something to a perceived standard (i.e. cooking gourmet meals) or that we are doing something we think is wrong except it is not in itself always wrong. Murder is always wrong. Eating a candy bar is not.

READ ROMANS 8:1-2. DOES GOD CONDEMN US?

So, if we are in Christ, and there is no condemnation for us, why do we feel guilty so often?

I spent many, many years feeling guilty over my past sins. Even though I was forgiven, and God had forgotten my sins, I could not. At every opportunity, I would drag up those old feelings and whack myself over the head with them. I shamed myself into behaving in a way I thought was correct.

After wasting many years thinking like this, I began to learn that confession (asking God for forgiveness for a sin) only needs to happen once. If we are sincere in our hearts, then we are forgiven.

READ COLOSSIANS 1:13-14. WHAT ARE WE RESCUED FROM?

---

[10] McGee, Robert S. *The Search for Significance: Seeing Your True Worth Through God's Eyes.* Abridged Version. Thomas Nelson, Inc. 2012. Audible.

WHO GIVES US REDEMPTION AND FORGIVENESS FOR OUR SINS?

WHAT DOES JOHN 8:44-45 CALL SATAN? WHAT ARE HIS CHARACTER-
ISTICS?

If our guilt is based on lies, then we are listening to Satan.

Robert S. McGee says that guilt makes us feel worthless, unworthy,
and that it withers the spirit.[11] Guilt leads us to rebellion and
isolation.

CONVICTION

Conviction, on the other hand, is not intended to lower our self-
worth or cause anxiety and guilt. Instead, conviction shows us that
our behavior is not lining up with God's truth.[12] Conviction should
lead us to repentance.

READ THE FOLLOWING VERSES ABOUT CONVICTION. MAKE A NOTE OF
WHAT CONVICTION IS AND HOW PEOPLE RESPONDED.

ACTS 2:36-41

ACTS 16:14-15

---

[11] McGee, Robert S. *The Search for Significance: Seeing Your True Worth Through
God's Eyes.* Abridged Version. Thomas Nelson, Inc. 2012. Audible.

[12] McGee, Robert S. *The Search for Significance: Seeing Your True Worth Through
God's Eyes.* Abridged Version. Thomas Nelson, Inc. 2012. Audible.

The people who heard Peter's sermon in Acts 2 were convicted. Those who accepted his message believed and were baptized (v41).

The same thing happened to Lydia in Acts 16. She believed, and her entire household was baptized. How do you suppose the rest of her household heard about the message? Very likely it was through her!

Conviction leads to a changed heart

The Thessalonians also heard and believed. Then they put their faith into practice so much that they became an example to the surrounding cities and region.

SOURCES OF CONVICTION

Conviction can come about through:

1. Preaching (Acts 2:14-41)
2. Holy Spirit (Romans 8:5-10)
3. Scripture (2 Timothy 3:15-17)
4. Prophecy (1 Corinthians 14:24-25)

In Acts 2:14-41, Peter preached to his fellow Israelites by explaining who Jesus really was and what they had done to persecute him was all part of the fulfillment of Scripture. His sermon "cut them to the heart" (v37).

The same can still happen today. There have been many times in my life where the words of a sermon, book, or Bible study have cut me to the core and revealed an area of my life where I needed to confess and change.

The Holy Spirit is another source of conviction. In Lydia's story from Acts 16, verse 14 in the NIV says, "The Lord opened her heart." Whether the process starts with words from a sermon, book, music, friend, etc., it is the Spirit that enables our hearts to be open.

Romans 8:5-10 talks about how when we have our minds set on what the Spirit desires, we are governed by the Spirit. We can see evidence of this in our lives because of the life and peace brought by the Spirit.

Scripture teaches us and shows us the principles to live by (see 2 Timothy 3:14-17). It points out areas where we need to change by the Spirit's power.

WHAT DOES 1 CORINTHIANS 14:24-25 SAY CAN HAPPEN WHEN PEOPLE ARE PROPHESYING?

WHAT IS "LAID BARE" ACCORDING TO VERSE 25?

I realize that prophecy can be confusing in the modern church. Some churches teach a powerless view on prophecy. Others speak in terms of prophecy and lead the believer by manipulative words instead.

In 1 Corinthians 12:7-11, Paul outlines the different manifestations of the Spirit and prophecy is included. Then, in 2 Peter 1:20-21, Peter tells us the source of prophecy:

- Prophecy is not from the prophet's interpretation.
- Prophecy does not originate from human will.
- Prophecy is spoken from God by the Holy Spirit through humans.

READ 1 CORINTHIANS 14:3 AND FILL IN THE BLANKS BELOW BASED ON PAUL'S TEACHING.

"But the one who prophesies speaks to people for their

_____, _____, and

_____."

Although, we do not have time to dig deeper into what modern day prophecy looks like, I do encourage you to "not treat prophecies with contempt," as Paul said in 1 Thessalonians 5:20. Instead, follow the Berean Jews' example from Acts 17:11 and examine scriptures to see if what I have represented here is true and to learn more about the topic of prophecy.

PERSONAL REFLECTION: THINK ABOUT THE PASSAGES YOU'VE READ AS PART OF TODAY'S LESSON. WHAT AREAS IN YOUR LIFE DO YOU FEEL FALSE GUILT IS HOLDING YOU BACK? ARE THERE AREAS OF YOUR LIFE WHERE THE SPIRIT IS LEADING YOU TO REPENTANCE?

PERSONALIZE ONE VERSE FROM TODAY'S LESSON.

DAY 4: ACTS OF THE FLESH

In session 3 we talked about how our flesh or sinful nature is in direct opposition with the Spirit and His work to transform us and our minds.

READ GALATIANS 5:19-21. CIRCLE THE WORDS THAT STAND OUT THE MOST TO YOU.

The acts of the flesh are obvious: sexual immorality, impurity and debauchery; idolatry and witchcraft; hatred, discord, jealousy, fits of rage, selfish ambition, dissensions, factions and envy; drunkenness, orgies, and the like. I warn you, as I did before, that those who live like this will not inherit the kingdom of God.

WHAT STRONG WARNING DOES PAUL GIVE THE GALATIANS?

This list of the acts of the flesh is not a complete list. Given Paul's strong warning about the acts of the flesh, let's look at a few that can become stumbling blocks to our progress in changing our thinking.

PRIDE

Although pride is not called out in the passage from Galatians, it is mentioned many times in Scripture.

When scripture talks about pride, it is not talking about the pride you have in your child when they do well at school or in a sport. It is talking about the type of pride that results in one thinking better of themselves than others. It is referring to the type of pride that is accompanied by conceit, disdain, haughtiness, and arrogance (see Jeremiah 48:29).

WHAT DOES PSALMS 101:5 SAY ABOUT PRIDE?

HOW DOES PROVERBS 16:5 DESCRIBE GOD'S VIEW ON PRIDE?

Luke 1:51 in the NIV says, "[God] has performed mighty deeds with his arm; he has **scattered those who are proud in their inmost thoughts.**"

So, these verses make it very clear that pride is high on God's hit list. Pride produces warped thoughts in our hearts and sin in our lives (Proverbs 21:4).

> *Pride produces warped thoughts in our hearts and sin in our lives*

WHAT DO THE FOLLOWING VERSES SAY ABOUT THE EFFECT OF OUR PRIDE?

DEUTERONOMY 8:12-14

2 CHRONICLES 32:25

PSALM 10:4

PROVERBS 18:12

Pride keeps us from seeking God. It keeps us from remembering God. It ignores kindness and causes our downfall. It keeps us from seeing and meeting the needs of others.

SELFISH AMBITION

One of the acts of the flesh listed in Galatians 5 includes selfish ambition.

READ PHILIPPIANS 2:3-4. WHAT DO THESE VERSES SAY WE SHOULD NOT DO?

ACCORDING TO THESE VERSES, WHAT IS THE OPPOSITE OF SELFISH AMBITION?

I used to think "selfish ambition" purely meant being selfish. Then, one day the word "ambition" jumped off the page at me. Our American culture praises ambition. I always thought ambition was a good thing—and I had an abundance of it.

One of my deepest ambitions went unfulfilled year after year. I didn't understand why God never granted me the dream to be a manager in my career. I had come close a few times—even held some of the responsibilities at one point. But, it fell short of my goal.

Then I began to ask Him what he thought about this dream. Over time, through prayer and continuing to study His Word, He made it very clear to me that my pursuit of this "dream" was actually selfish ambition. I wanted to make a name for myself and I wanted to use the gifts He gave me (leadership, organization, administration) for my own purposes. My motive was not pure.

He also revealed to me that the fulfillment of my dream in the way I envisioned would be very harmful to me. It would have taken my eyes from His plan and it would have caused me great pain.

I am thankful that God worked to correct my vision of this ambition and use of these gifts. He is now molding it into some amazing things that bring glory to Him.

PERSONAL REFLECTION: IS THERE A DREAM, GOAL, OR AMBITION IN YOUR LIFE WHERE YOU ARE NOT SEEKING GOD'S COUNSEL? IF SO, TAKE A MINUTE TO WRITE OUT A PRAYER ABOUT IT.

The NIV uses the phrase "fits of rage" in the list of acts of the flesh from Galatians 5:19-21. The NLT says "outbursts of anger". The CEB uses "losing your temper".

I don't know about you, but I have had outbursts of anger, fits of rage, and I have lost my temper more than once in my life. Certain times of the month I may seem more prone to this. Yet, the truth is that my short fuse is likely because I have either allowed myself to be easily offended or quickly provoked.

WHAT DOES PROVERBS 19:11 SAY ABOUT A PERSON WHO OVERLOOKS AN OFFENSE?

WHAT DOES ECCLESIASTES 7:9 SAY ABOUT WHERE AND HOW WE CAN BE PROVOKED? WHERE DOES ANGER RESIDE?

Ephesians 4:26-27 says that we are not to sin in our anger. Again, we have a choice of how to deal with our anger. It is not a sin to get angry. However, we can choose the wrong way to deal with our anger.

WHAT GUIDANCE DO WE GET FROM THE FOLLOWING VERSES TO HELP US LEARN HOW TO HANDLE OUR ANGER?

PROVERBS 12:16

PROVERBS 15:1

JAMES 1:19-20

We can deal with our anger in several ways:

1. We can overlook the insult and choose not to be easily offended.
2. We can stay calm and speak with gentleness.
3. We can listen instead of speaking.
4. We can choose to be slow to anger. For some people, counting to ten slowly in their mind helps them overcome the initial rush of anger.

Please do not hear what I am not saying. When our anger stems from deep rooted pain caused by abuse or neglect, I am **not** suggesting we overlook what was done to us or that we bypass the healing process by ignoring the offense.

I am talking about when our anger is not justified.

PERSONALIZE ONE OF THE VERSES FROM TODAY'S LESSON BELOW.

DAY 5: EMOTION

Many of us struggle with controlling our emotions, so our feelings can be a stumbling block in our journey to changing our thinking.

For some of you, just reading the word "emotion" brings a whole host of emotions to the surface. For others, you may be rolling your eyes. Despite your initial reaction, I am asking you to be open to learning something new, even if you have already learned how to control your emotions.

My journal is filled with questions like:

Why can't I control my emotions?
Why can I just not care so much?
Why do I have an over-abundance of emotions?

For many years I focused on my emotions themselves. I wanted to know why I was feeling the way I was or what I could do about it.

Deep down, I just wished my emotions would go away. They seemed to cause me more harm than good.

My journey towards changing my thinking started with a deep desire to change my emotions. For years I studied books about topics like self-esteem, emotional intelligence, insecurity, and other specific emotions. While I learned something from each book, I did not truly have a lasting victory in this area until I understood the principles outlined in today's lesson.

WARNING SIGN

"Feelings are indicators, not dictators." –Lysa TerKeurst, *Unglued*[13]

Read that quote again. Yeah, I didn't quite understand the depth of meaning behind those words for the first thirty times I read them, either.

The point is that our emotions serve a purpose. They exist to serve us, to warn us, and not to control us. Sometimes those emotions are red herrings for what is really going on. Sometimes they are symptoms of the real problem. Sometimes they are intensified by hormones, health conditions, stress, or lack of sleep.

I wrote it in my journal this way, "My supercharged emotions are a nudge from God that I need to stop and process something in my life."

DO YOU STRUGGLE TO CONTROL YOUR EMOTIONS? HOW DOES KNOWING THAT THEY ARE A WARNING SIGN CHANGE YOUR PERSPECTIVE?

---

[13] TerKeurst, Lysa. *Unglued: Making Wise Choices in the Midst of Raw Emotions.* Grand Rapids, MI: Zondervan, 2012. 7 Aug. 2012. Kindle.

Emotions come from thoughts rooted in what we believe to be true

I could go on for pages—perhaps even filling an entire book about the root of our emotions, but I'll spare you and cut to the chase.

Our emotions come from our thoughts. Let me say that again, the root of our emotions come from what is going on in our thought life, our heart.

Robert S. McGee states it this way, "Destructive emotions come from destructive thoughts that come from false beliefs and are energized by life situations."[14]

That's right. The conversations in our heads have the power to either blow up or diffuse our emotions. What we think about ourselves and others can dramatically affect our emotions.

Negative thoughts can cause our emotions to spiral out of control. Positive thoughts can help us gain perspective and see truth.

WHAT DOES PROVERBS 12:25 SAY ABOUT ANXIETY?

WHAT DOES PROVERBS 15:15 TELL YOU ABOUT NEGATIVE THINKING VERSUS POSITIVE THINKING?

ACCORDING TO ROMANS 8:6, WHAT HAPPENS TO THE MIND GOVERNED BY THE FLESH? HOW IS THAT DIFFERENT FROM THE MIND GOVERNED BY THE SPIRIT?

---

[14] McGee, Robert S. *The Search for Significance: Seeing Your True Worth Through God's Eyes.* Abridged Version. Thomas Nelson, Inc. 2012. Audible.

WHAT DOES PROVERBS 15:13 TELL US ABOUT THE DIFFERENCE BETWEEN A HAPPY HEART AND HEARTACHE?

WHAT FURTHER INSIGHT DOES PROVERBS 17:22 PROVIDE?

WHAT CAN WE LEARN FROM ISAIAH 26:3 ABOUT THE POSITIVE THINKER (THOSE WHOSE MINDS ARE STEADFAST)?

LIST EVERYTHING THAT PHILIPPIANS 4:8-9 SAYS WE SHOULD THINK ABOUT.

Our thoughts can make us happy or heartbroken, cheerful or crushed, peaceful or in turmoil. As we learn to change our thinking to what is noble, pure, right, excellent, and praiseworthy, our emotions will follow.

CONTROLLING EMOTIONS

Although our initial reaction to a situation or conversation might trigger certain emotions, we can choose to not give away control of our emotions. We do not have to act on our feelings.

I'm not suggesting that we stuff our emotions or disregard them. Even though we can still feel our emotions, we can stop them from controlling us.

We do not have to act on our feelings

READ ECCLESIASTES 3:1-8. WHAT CAN WE LEARN ABOUT OUR EMOTIONS FROM THIS PASSAGE?

WHAT DO YOU BELIEVE IS A HEALTHY PERSPECTIVE ABOUT EMOTIONS?

WHAT DOES PROVERBS 29:11 SAY?

How can we control our emotions? The answer is very similar to how we can control our thoughts. We must first learn to recognize our emotions. Then we hold our emotions up to the truth of Scripture and we seek guidance from the Holy Spirit for how to deal with our emotions.

This is an ongoing process that takes time. There will be days where we are successful and fully experience self-control and peace. There will also be days where we fall short.

Another factor in learning to control our emotions is to deal with our past hurts, habits, and hang ups. If we deny or try to hide deep emotional hurts, we will be more likely to give our feelings full vent.

PERSONAL REFLECTION: TAKE A MINUTE TO INVENTORY YOUR EMOTIONS. DO YOU HAVE SOME UNRESOLVED HURT IN YOUR LIFE? IS THERE SOME EMOTION YOU NEED TO LET GO? PRAY AND ASK THE HOLY

SPIRIT TO SHOW YOU. THEN JOT DOWN A FEW NOTES ABOUT WHAT THE
NEXT STEPS ARE THAT YOU NEED TO TAKE.

PICK A VERSE FROM TODAY AND PERSONALIZE IT.

But seek first his kingdom and his righteousness, and all these things will be given to you as well. Therefore do not worry about tomorrow, for tomorrow will worry about itself. Each day has enough trouble of its own. –Matthew 5:33-34

_____ left unchecked leads to _____.

_____ left unchecked leads to _____.

_____ left unchecked leads to _____.

FEAR

What can we do about our fear? (Isaiah 41:10)

1. Remember God is _____ _____. ("I am

   _____ _____.")

2. Remember God is _____ _____. ("I am

   _____ _____")

3. God is our _____ of _____.

   ("I will _____ you and _____ you")

4. Remember God is our _____. ("I will

   _____ you")

5. Remember God _____ us from our fear if

   we _____ Him. (Psalm 34:4, Psalm 56:3)

WORRY

Matthew 6:25-34 tells us the reasons why we should not worry:

1. We can trust that _____ will _____

   for us because He _____ for the birds of

   the air and the grass of the field. (v26, 30)

2. We are _____ to God. (v26,30)

3. Worrying is a _____ of _____. (v27)

4. Worrying will not _____ the

   _____. (v27)

5. Worrying is the _____ way, not _____

   way. (v31,33)

6. _____ way involves _____ His

   _____. (v33)

ANXIETY

Casting our _____ on God requires a _____

_____. (1 Peter 5:6-7)

Casting involves _____ and vehemently

_____ our anxieties from our

_____. (1 Peter 5:6-7)

God _____ us when we _____ our

_____ on Him. (Psalm 55:22)

God gives us peace beyond our _____

when we turn our anxiety into _____ and thanks-

giving. (Philippians 4:6-7)

_____

_____

_____

The beginning of anxiety is the end of faith, and the beginning of true faith is the end of anxiety. –George Mueller

In Session 4, I introduced the concept of the vicious cycle of fear, worry, and anxiety. There is so much more to these topics and how they relate to transforming our minds. Fear, worry, and anxiety can trap us in a cycle of thinking that leaves no room for thoughts of God and His presence, provision, and peace.

At the end of each day this week, we will learn one of the names of God and how His name can help counteract our fear, worry, and anxiety.

DAY 1: WHAT IF

I am a planner. In some ways this can be a very good trait. I can come up with contingency plans in my career for various outcomes. "What if" the product doesn't arrive on time? "What if" our customer backs out? "What if" our computer systems crash? "What if" our staff is out on vacation? I see all the possibilities and am prepared to deal with them all. Even so, this type of thinking can go overboard. We can become paranoid or just stressed out by thinking through too many scenarios.

"What if" thoughts can be dangerous in our personal lives, thought lives, and in our relationships, too. "What if" my unborn child has a birth defect? "What if" I miscarry again? "What if" my husband no longer finds me attractive? "What if" my marriage fails? "What if" he turns out to be just like my dad? "What if" my child gets bullied in school? "What if" my child gets bad grades? "What if" I can't kick this addiction?

Do you feel the heaviness weighing on you just from reading these "what if's"? I do.

PERSONAL REFLECTION: WHAT ARE SOME OF THE "WHAT IF'S" THAT PLAGUE YOU?

READ PHILIPPIANS 4:6-7. WHAT IS THE SOLUTION FOR OUR "WHAT IF" (ANXIOUS) THINKING?

WHEN SHOULD WE DO WHAT PHILIPPIANS 4:6-7 SAYS?

That's right. In every situation, circumstance, and event, we can turn our "what if's" into prayers and petitions.

When we take our "what if's" to God, we must believe He will answer

Think about the word petition. In the legal system, a petition is a thought-out and documented request for some action or judgment. When a petition is submitted, it is with hopeful anticipation that the desired outcome occurs.

So, instead of worrying about our circumstances, let's present our worries and "what if's" to God in hopeful anticipation of a desired outcome. Believe that He will answer.

WHAT ATTITUDE SHOULD ACCOMPANY OUR PRAYERS AND PETITIONS (v6)?

God won't always answer our prayers and petitions in the way we want. Regardless, He does ask that we approach Him with an attitude of thanksgiving. When we start with gratitude, it helps lift some of the worry off our shoulders and opens our hearts to trusting His plan.

TIP: Start your prayers with gratitude.

What does thanksgiving look like when we have "what if's" to present to God?

Let's go back to our example of the child with the bad grades. We could say something like this: "Lord, thank you that my son lives in a country where education is valued and that he can learn. Give me wisdom for how to talk to him about his grades. Help him to have the desire to do well in school. Regardless, of the outcome, God, I trust you."

Verse 7 says that "the peace of God" will guard our hearts and
minds. Isn't that exactly what we need when we are worried? We
need minds and hearts that are protected from the frenzy of worry.

JEHOVAH JIREH (THE LORD WILL PROVIDE) [15]

The root of most of my worry and anxiety comes from a fear that I
will not have what I need. When I faced job loss in early 2016, my
fears were about how long it would take to get a new job and "what
if" we depleted our savings before the new job came.

Another example: "What if" my child has a birth defect? This thought
might be based on a fear of how I will handle this situation. Where
will the money come from for her medical bills? I feel so helpless that
I can't fix this for her.

"What ifs" are an attempt to anticipate a lack of provision and
preemptively plan how *we* will provide for ourselves instead of
trusting *God's* provision.

READ THE FOLLOWING PASSAGES AND NOTE THE SITUATION AND GOD'S
PROVISION.

	SITUATION	GOD'S PROVISION
GENESIS 22:1-14 key verses: 7-8, 13		
JOHN 6:1-13 key verses: 5, 9, 12		

---

[15] "What are the different names of God and what do they mean?" Got Questions
Ministries, n.d. Web. 24 Apr. 2016.

In Genesis, God provided another sacrifice for Abraham so that he didn't have to sacrifice his only son. In John, Jesus provided food for 5,000 people from five loaves of bread and two fish.

If God purposefully provided in each of these situations, will he not provide for you?

WHAT DOES PHILIPPIANS 4:19 SAY THAT HELPS FURTHER YOUR UNDERSTANDING OF JEHOVAH JIREH (THE LORD WILL PROVIDE)?

PICK A VERSE FROM TODAY AND PERSONALIZE IT.

DAY 2: WHY

When something unexpected or traumatic happens to us, we often ask the question "why". Sometimes, our circumstances are the consequences of our actions, like an alcoholic that has liver problems. Conversely, there are many circumstances outside of our control, like the man who has liver problems but never drank.

Take the example of infertility. A couple struggling with this may ask: "Why can't I have children? What did I do that caused me not to be able to have children? Was it because I partied in college?" There was nothing the couple did that caused them to be infertile.

The truth is that sometimes bad, unexplainable stuff happens to us or in our lives.

When we are too focused on why we are dealing with a difficult circumstance our thoughts become anxious. We get stuck in our "why's". We feel alone, and we want someone or something to blame. We feel like we will have to carry this suffering forever. We believe that no one knows how much we are suffering.

SUFFERING WELL

READ 2 CORINTHIANS 12:1-10.

According to Moody Bible Commentary, the "man in Christ" is Paul. The "third heaven" in this passage means the part of heaven where Jesus and God are. In this passage, Paul is telling the believers at Corinth that fourteen years ago he had a vision or revelation directly from the throne of God and Paul was given a thorn in his flesh which most scholars believe was a physical ailment. He was also undergoing a spiritual battle ("messenger of Satan to torment me").[16]

HOW DID PAUL FEEL ABOUT THE "THORN" IN HIS FLESH AND WHAT DID HE DO ABOUT IT (V7-8)?

WHAT WAS GOD'S RESPONSE (V9)?

BECAUSE OF GOD'S RESPONSE, WHAT NEW MINDSET DID PAUL DEVELOP (V10)?

Paul pleaded with God to take away his ailment and remove the spiritual battle in which he was engaged. However, God did not remove Paul from his circumstances and He did not free him from his trial.

---

[16] Rydelnik, Michael, et al. "2 Corinthians 12:1-8". *The Moody Bible Commentary*. Chicago: Moody Press, 2014. Accessed 1 February 2018. Olive Tree Bible Software.

Joy is a choice

Yet, Paul responded with a new attitude. He trusted that God's grace was enough, and that God would still work through his weaknesses. Paul chose to view his trials with joy and remember that God was at work in those hardships.

READ 1 PETER 5:8-10. WHAT KIND OF MIND ARE WE TO HAVE DURING TRIALS AND WHY?

ACCORDING TO VERSE 10, WHAT HAPPENS AFTER A WHILE?

READ JAMES 1:2-5. WHAT HAPPENS TO US DURING TRIALS?

WHAT PROMISE CAN WE HOLD ON TO IN VERSE 5?

In each of the above passages, God is an active source of grace, strength, and wisdom. He uses trials to mature us and refine our faith. Furthermore, He never abandons us. He always sees exactly what we are going through and how hard it is. We are not alone.

EL ROI (GOD OF SEEING)[17]

In Genesis 16:1-14, Hagar is Sarah's (Sarai) maid servant. Abraham (Abram) sleeps with her and she gets pregnant. When Sarah mistreats her, she flees to the desert. Then an angel of the Lord appeared to her and asked her where she was going.

---

[17] "What are the different names of God and what do they mean?" Got Questions Ministries, n.d. Web. 24 Apr. 2016.

READ GENESIS 16:8-14. WHAT DID THE ANGEL TELL HAGAR TO DO?

WHAT PROMISES WERE MADE TO HAGAR?

WHAT DID HAGAR SAY IN VERSE 13?

God is the God who sees. He saw Hagar's misery and pain. He heard her cries. And He promised her that her descendants would be too numerous to count.

However, He did not promise that everything would be sunshine and roses. The prophecy in verse 12 is somewhat disturbing.

Still, for Hagar it was enough to know that God saw her situation.

READ THE FOLLOWING VERSES AND NOTE WHAT GOD SEES.

2 CHRONICLES 16:9

JOB 28:24

JOB 34:21

PSALM 33:13-15

God is the God who sees. He sees the pain you are going through. He feels your pain. He cares. Let your heart rest in the knowledge that God sees it all.

PERSONAL REFLECTION: WHAT STOOD OUT TO YOU THE MOST FROM TODAY'S LESSON? HOW CAN YOU APPLY THIS TO CURRENT OR FUTURE TRIALS IN YOUR LIFE?

PERSONALIZE ONE VERSE FROM TODAY'S LESSON.

DAY 3: WHAT WE WORRY ABOUT (PART 1)

So far this week, we've looked at our "what if" thinking and our "why" thinking. Now let's look at what we worry about.

WORTHLESS THINGS

Some of my worrying is over worthless things, like traffic. My daily commute is over an hour one way every day. Much of that commute time is spent sitting still or going very slowly on the freeway. I used to let this commute bother me. I was hyper-vigilant of other drivers, constantly afraid that someone was going to hit me.

Then one day it occurred to me that my fear and anxiety on that commute was raising my blood pressure and causing me to arrive at work physically stressed. I made the decision to stop worrying about things I could not control, like traffic.

ACCORDING TO MATTHEW 6:25-34, WHAT ARE SOME OF THE "WORTHLESS THINGS" WE WORRY ABOUT?

I used to worry a lot about my appearance. In middle school, a classmate made fun of the clothes I wore, because I only had one style of jeans. I internalized those words to the point of tracking what clothes I wore on a particular day. I made sure not to wear the same outfit on the same day of the week, all so no one would think I was poor.

I have since learned that worrying (thinking too much or in an unhealthy way) about my clothes or food or drink or the commute to work is truly a waste of time and energy. These things are some of the "worthless things" referred to in Psalm 119:37.

In the NIV, there is a footnote for Psalm 119:37 that says "life according to your word" could also mean "life in your way". By worrying about worthless things, we are distracted from living in God's Way.

Worry distracts us from living God's Way

PERSONAL REFLECTION: ARE THERE SOME "WORTHLESS THINGS" YOU ARE WORRYING ABOUT? IF SO, HOW HAVE THEY KEPT YOU FROM LIVING IN GOD'S WAY? TAKE A MINUTE TO PRAY AND ASK GOD TO HELP YOU LET GO OF WORRYING ABOUT THEM.

God is our strength in trouble. We can rely on Him to be our source of strength even when we do not understand our circumstances.

WHAT DOES PSALM 37:39 CALL GOD?

READ MATTHEW 19:26. WHAT DOES JESUS SAY ABOUT WHAT IS POSSIBLE?

HOW DOES KNOWING THIS BRING YOU COMFORT IN LIGHT OF YOUR CURRENT FEARS, WORRIES, AND ANXIETIES?

WHAT DOES PHILIPPIANS 4:13 SAY IS THE SOURCE OF OUR STRENGTH? WHAT CAN WE DO WITH THIS STRENGTH?

HOW MUCH FAITH DOES MATTHEW 17:20 SAY THAT WE NEED IN ORDER FOR NOTHING TO BE IMPOSSIBLE FOR US?

Faith is believing what He says is true even when we don't feel it

Faith is believing what He says is true even when we do not feel it. The next time you worry about things, remember that nothing is impossible for God and that He gives us the ability to do anything in his strength if we have faith.

---

[18]Jones, Jay. "Compound Names of Jehovah." *Preaching Points*. N.p., 27 Aug. 2010. Web. 24 Apr. 2016.

DAY 4: WHAT WE WORRY ABOUT (PART 2)

In my early twenties, I went through a very rebellious period in my life. I married a man who was not right for me. I moved to a foreign country. Then I put God up on a dusty shelf and sought my own way.

Though this rebellious period lasted only a few years, the things I did during that period shaped me. I picked up some bad habits, like placing a high importance on what others thought of me. This habit of worrying about what other people think of me became a heavy burden that weighed me down for many years.

In addition to some bad habits, I did some very sinful things. For many years, I thought about those sins. I confessed them, gave them to God, and in a short time, I would rip them back out of God's hands. I was forgiven, but I worried myself into a place where I experienced no freedom. My anxiety about my past was beginning to define my future.

OUR PAST

Perhaps you are like me. Perhaps you have done something in your past, or something was done to you, that causes you to repeatedly visit the past. Maybe it is something you have given over to God countless times, yet it always seems to haunt you.

For example, let's say a woman had an affair, then repented of it and received forgiveness from God and her spouse. Yet, she constantly worried about that affair or was overly fearful that she would fall into a new affair. The more time she spent thinking about it, the more her mind was set on it. Then she would be more likely to have another affair because she obsessed about it.

READ 2 CORINTHIANS 7:10. WHAT DO YOU THINK THIS MEANS?

There is a big difference between healthy self-evaluation (godly sorrow) and fear, worry, and anxiety. Healthy self-evaluation allows us to see the error of our ways. Then we turn from our ways and walk a new way. This is the essence of repentance.

PERSONAL REFLECTION: ARE YOU THINKING TOO MUCH ABOUT A PAST SIN? IF SO, HOW IS IT AFFECTING YOU AND YOUR RELATIONSHIPS?

READ PHILIPPIANS 3:13-14. WHAT DID PAUL DO ABOUT HIS PAST?

WHAT DID PAUL DO ABOUT HIS FUTURE?

It is only through letting go of our past that we can press on toward our future. This process can require counseling or self-evaluation and hard work to get through the issues. Eventually, there comes a time to forget. Let it go. Press on.

The Lord Who Heals. This name of God is so very relevant for those of us struggling with our past. God can heal us from it. It comes from Exodus 15:26.

READ EXODUS 15:22-27. WHAT HAPPENED TO THE ISRAELITES?

WHAT DID MOSES DO?

WHAT DID GOD ASK OF THE ISRAELITES (V26) AND WHAT DID HE PROMISE IN RETURN?

WHY DO YOU THINK GOD SAID, "I AM THE LORD, WHO HEALS YOU"?

I find it interesting that after God provided water for the Israelites to drink and He instructs them to keep his commands and do what is right in His eyes, He tells them He is their healer. I don't know why He says this. Allow me to speculate for a moment.

In verse 24, the Israelites were grumbling again. They had just walked across the Red Sea on dry land three days ago. Three. Not seven days, not a month. Three days.

That speaks volumes about their heart condition. They were joyful and singing when things were going right. When their circumstances changed, they lost faith and grumbled.

---

[19] "What are the different names of God and what do they mean?" Got Questions Ministries, n.d. Web. 24 Apr. 2016.

I think God reminded them of the diseases in Egypt and of His power to heal their hearts, so they would focus their thoughts back on Him.

Let's look at a few other verses about The Lord Who Heals.

READ PSALM 103:2-5. WHAT DOES VERSE 3 SAY ABOUT GOD?

Notice the words "forgives all your sins" precedes the words "heals all your diseases".

READ MARK 2:1-12. WHAT WAS THE FIRST THING JESUS SAID TO THE MAN?

WHY DO YOU THINK HE SAID THIS?

HOW DOES THIS PASSAGE RELATE TO PSALM 103:3?

Jesus forgave the paralyzed man's sins. He dealt with the heart condition before dealing with the man's physical condition. All the paralyzed man had to do was show up.

True healing begins in the heart

True healing of any kind begins in the heart. This is why God told the Israelites He is the Lord Who Heals.

When you feel stuck in your past, remember that God is The Lord Who Heals. He first forgives your sins and then He sets about healing you from your condition. There is no need to worry or stay in your past. Let Him do this work in you.

TAKE A MINUTE TO PRAY ABOUT THE SITUATION YOU WROTE DOWN IN THE PERSONAL REFLECTION QUESTION ON PAGE 86. IS GOD SHOWING YOU STEPS YOU NEED TO TAKE TOWARDS FORGIVENESS AND HEALING?

PERSONALIZE A VERSE FROM TODAY'S LESSON.

DAY 5: ILLUSION OF CONTROL

When life seems to spin completely out of control, some of us tend to morph into control freak mode without realizing it. At work or in a true crisis, this can be a good trait. We are the ones taking charge and doling out orders until the crisis is over.

Unfortunately, there are many things in life that we simply cannot control. We cannot control the unexpected loss of a loved one. We cannot control a health diagnosis for ourselves or those close to us. We cannot control an unexpected job loss.

So, what do we do when life hands us a giant pile of lemons?

For me, I spent many years trying to control and order my life in such a way that I thought I could minimize any aspect of my life feeling out of control. I would plan my driving route to work so I would run into the least amount of traffic as possible—not because I wanted to get there faster, but because I was consumed with the fear of getting in an accident. The only thing that would soothe my fear was doing something that made me feel like I was in control.

I also spent a lot of time thinking up rules that would affair proof my marriage. Some of those rules, like not going to lunch alone with a guy from work, seemed very good on the surface except my motivation was off track. I wanted to believe that I could control circumstances to the point that it would be impossible for me or my husband to have an affair.

Both examples only gave me the illusion of having control over things that I could never control. I could not have done anything to prevent a car from hitting me. Likewise, there is no guaranteed way to affair proof my marriage.

PERSONAL REFLECTION: CAN YOU RELATE? ARE THERE THINGS IN YOUR LIFE THAT GIVE YOU THE ILLUSION OF CONTROL?

Why do we try to plan and orchestrate outcomes that we cannot truly control? Because, even when we have the illusion of control we feel safe or secure.

At the root of these controlling tendencies and unhealthy thinking is a trust issue. We don't trust God to truly take care of us no matter what happens.

READ THE FOLLOWING VERSES AND NOTE WHAT THEY SAY ABOUT TRUST AND ABOUT GOD.

PSALM 28:6-7

PSALM 56:3

PROVERBS 3:5-6

PROVERBS 28:25

PROVERBS 29:25

God keeps us safe when we trust Him. He helps us. We will prosper. We do not have to be afraid. He smooths out the rough patches in the road before us when we trust Him.

WHO IS IN CONTROL?

God is in control. Yes, God is in control of everything. Who causes it to rain? Who created the world and everything in it? Who put you in the place where you live at this time in history?

WHAT DOES ROMANS 13:1 SAY ABOUT THE GOVERNMENT AND RULING AUTHORITIES?

WHAT DOES ISAIAH 55:8-11 SAY ABOUT GOD'S THOUGHTS?

WHAT DO YOU THINK VERSE 11 MEANS?

READ ISAIAH 45:5-7. WHAT DOES VERSE 5 SAY ABOUT GOD?

LIST ALL OF THE THINGS FROM THESE VERSES THAT GOD CONTROLS.

So, if God is in control, then why do we spend so much time and energy trying to control the things that He is handling?

JEHOVAH-SHALOM (THE LORD OUR PEACE)[20]

The answer to our controlling behavior is: surrender. When we surrender to Him, we will experience His peace.

WHERE DOES COLOSSIANS 3:15 SAY THAT THE PEACE OF CHRIST RULES?

WHAT DOES ROMANS 15:13 SAY IS REQUIRED OF US IN ORDER TO BE FILLED WITH JOY AND PEACE?

READ ISAIAH 26:3. WHO DOES GOD KEEP IN PERFECT PEACE?

It takes a steadfast, unwavering, firmly fixed, and determined mind to trust God and stay in His perfect peace. When we catch ourselves trying to control our circumstances or things that are beyond our control, let's stop and pray and surrender that need for control to the One in control.

PICK ONE VERSE FROM THIS LESSON AND PERSONALIZE IT BELOW.

Surrender the need to control to the One in control

---

[20] "What are the different names of God and what do they mean?" Got Questions Ministries, n.d. Web. 24 Apr. 2016.

SESSION 5: LOVE ONE ANOTHER (& YOURSELF)

A new command I give you: Love one another. As I have loved you, so you must love one another. By this everyone will know that you are my disciples, if you love one another. –John 13:34-35

SELF-CENTEREDNESS

_____ _____ (loving ourselves _____

_____) keeps us from loving others.

The _____ for self-centeredness is

_____. (Philippians 2:3-4)

LOW SELF-ESTEEM

_____ _____ (loving ourselves _____

_____) keeps us from loving others.

God gives us _____ and _____ us to

_____ them. (Matthew 25:14-30)

Our fear of _____ needs to _____ our fear

of _____. (Matthew 25:14-30)

HEALTHY SELF-IMAGE

A _____ self-image (loving ourselves _____

_____) enables us to live out God's _____ and to use

the gifts He has given us. (Romans 12:3-8)

When we set our _____ on _____ things,

_____ things become less important. (Colossians 3:1-4)

You are more than halfway through this study! Congratulations on persevering and growing. I am so proud of you for sticking with such a difficult and deep-rooted topic.

Being transformed by the renewing of our minds takes time and effort. Things won't change overnight. Your feelings won't always line up with your thoughts.

Holley Gerth, in her life growth guide *You're Already Amazing*, said:

> *Updating a thought pattern is like learning a new habit, and it can take six months to a year for that process to be complete. The key is to continue repeating our new ways of thinking even though our emotions don't align with them.*[21]

As I sit here writing this, I have just had one of *those* weeks. You know the kind. No matter what you do and no matter how hard you fight to gain ground, the enemy tries to take some of that ground back. That was my week. Even though I didn't feel like I was doing a good job, I repeated positive words to myself in my head. I pulled up verses on my phone while at work. I texted my circle of closest friends for prayer support.

Then I had this thought: a situation at work left me feeling down, but only for part of a day. In the past, I would have fed that down feeling until it turned into self-recrimination and depression. It would have taken me weeks to bounce back instead of less than twenty-four hours.

It is so very important to our growth to remember the victories no matter how small. Write them down. Look back at them when you feel down or discouraged about your progress. Maybe you used to be oblivious to your thoughts. Now you are learning to evaluate your thoughts. Maybe you used to eat a carton of ice cream after a difficult day. Now you see the connection with your thoughts and make a positive choice instead.

Whatever those victories are, celebrate them!

---

[21] Gerth, Holley. "What's True No Matter How We Feel." *You're Already Amazing Life Growth Guide: Embracing Who You Are, Becoming All God Created You To Be.* Grand Rapids, Michigan: Revell, 2016. 57. Print.

THINK ABOUT THE CHANGES YOU HAVE ALREADY MADE BECAUSE OF WHAT YOU'RE LEARNING. USE THE SPACE BELOW TO WRITE DOWN SOME VICTORIES TO CELEBRATE. EVEN IF YOU DON'T THINK YOU HAVE ANY VICTORIES YET, ASK GOD TO SHOW YOU THE ONES YOU CAN'T SEE.

_____

_____

_____

_____

_____

_____

_____

_____

_____

_____

_____

_____

_____

As I have learned to deal with my thinking, I found there were thought patterns that dramatically affected my relationships with others. Only when I began to deal with those faulty thought patterns, did I see changes in my interpersonal relationships at home, in my extended family, and even in the workplace.

This week, we will look at four faulty thought patterns that drive us to:

1. Please people
2. Control people
3. Assume we know what others think
4. Hide our authentic self from others

Then we will look at how to deal with conflict.

DAY 1: PEOPLE PLEASER

As I sit down to write this lesson, my own tendencies to be a people pleaser are very fresh in my mind. Just a few days ago, I went to a negative place with my thoughts. My client was pushing our project team to start working overtime in the evenings and weekends, even though we are only two months into an eighteen-month project. The war within me started. I knew that it was not good for my health to agree to do this, yet I really wanted my client to be happy.

The more I thought about the situation, the angrier I became. Then I started to feel down about myself. If I didn't work extra hours, even though I knew it was bad for me, my client might think I'm not working hard. If I didn't keep my client happy, then they might say bad things about me. If that happened, then I might not get good marks on my next review.

Meanwhile, I was stuck on my work assignment. I couldn't figure out how to do something and instead of staying calm and working through the problem, I panicked because I was afraid of what my client would say if I could not complete this task on time.

The truth of the situation is that I allowed what I thought other people were thinking about me to dictate how I felt about myself.

Then, I came across these two quotes:

We try to find our significance and security through others' opinions and approval of us.[22] *–Robert S. McGee*

In the situation at my job, I was unhappy and upset because I knew that writing this study was a significantly more important use of my evenings and weekends than the project at work. I also knew that having an appropriate work-life balance was important for my health, well-being, and the well-being of my marriage. In the end, I decided it was more important to do what I knew to be right (work-life balance) than to focus so much energy on pleasing people.

WHAT STOOD OUT MOST TO YOU IN THE QUOTES FROM ROBERT S. MCGEE?

APPROVAL ADDICT

What does a people pleaser or approval addict look like?

You might be an approval addict if you:

1. Say "yes" to everyone even when you know it is not good for you.
2. Are sensitive to criticism.
3. Cannot accept praise for the good things you do.
4. Isolate yourself from others.
5. Get your identity from a group of friends instead of God.
6. Rescue others from the consequences of their actions (co-dependency).
7. Spend much of your thought life thinking or worrying about what other people think of you.
8. Stuff your emotions.
9. Find it hard to give or receive love.

---

[22] McGee, Robert S. *The Search for Significance: Seeing Your True Worth Through God's Eyes.* Abridged Version. Thomas Nelson, Inc. 2012. Audible.

PERSONAL REFLECTION: CAN YOU IDENTIFY WITH ANY OF THE PEOPLE PLEASING TENDENCIES LISTED ABOVE? IF SO, CIRCLE THE NUMBER OF THE ONE(S) YOU STRUGGLE WITH THE MOST. THEN TAKE A MINUTE TO WRITE OUT A PRAYER ASKING THE HOLY SPIRIT TO HELP YOU RECOGNIZE WHEN YOU ARE DOING THIS AND HOW TO CHANGE.

PEOPLE PLEASERS FROM THE BIBLE

READ JOHN 12:42-43. THE JEWISH LEADERS IN THIS PASSAGE BELIEVED IN JESUS. WHAT KEPT THEM FROM ADMITTING THEIR BELIEF?

WRITE VERSE 43 IN THE SPACE BELOW.

The Jewish leaders were so afraid of the Pharisees that they sought to please them more than God.

READ MARK 15:11-15 AND MATTHEW 27:11-26. WHAT DID PILATE KNOW ABOUT JESUS?

WHAT DID THE CHIEF PRIESTS AND ELDERS WANT?

WHAT DID PILATE DO IN THE END AND WHY (MARK 15:15, MATTHEW 27:24-26)?

WHO WAS PILATE TRYING TO PLEASE?

Mark 15:15 in the NIV says that Pilate wanted to "satisfy the crowd". The NLT uses the word "pacify". The Message says, "Pilate gave the crowd what it wanted".

When Pilate heard the case against Jesus, he knew what the chief priests and elders were up to. Even though he knew that Jesus was innocent, he gave in to what the crowd wanted.

READ ACTS 12:1-3. WHAT DID KING HEROD DO IN VERSES 1 & 2?

WHY DID KING HEROD SEIZE PETER?

In each of these examples, the motivation was to please a certain group of people. In the case of Pilate, Herod, and Felix, their actions caused the death of Jesus and James as well as the imprisonment of Peter and Paul.

When we place too much importance on pleasing others, we can get ourselves and even other people into a bad situation.

PLEASING GOD NOT PEOPLE

So, what should we do then? How do we fight our people pleasing nature?

READ THE FOLLOWING PASSAGES AND NOTE WHAT HAPPENS WHEN WE PLEASE GOD VERSUS WHEN WE PLEASE MAN.

	PLEASING GOD	PLEASING MAN
PSALM 118:5-9		
PROVERBS 29:25-26		
ISAIAH 2:22		
JEREMIAH 17:5-8		

Why should we fear other people? What can they really do to us? God is in control. God protects us and gives us strength. We can trust Him. He is worthy of our fear. He is worthy of having us try to please Him.

WHAT HAPPENS, ACCORDING TO PROVERBS 16:7, WHEN WE MAKE IT A PRIORITY TO PLEASE GOD?

The verses from Galatians and Proverbs really hit home for me in my situation at work. I would much rather serve Jesus by writing this study or making my husband a priority in my life, than to disregard Him and please my client instead.

When we keep ourselves from being entrapped or ensnared by people pleasing, God is the one who keeps us safe and gets justice for us (Proverbs 29:25-26). He can cause those people we're worried about to make peace with us.

How do we please God? We walk in a manner worthy of Him (Col. 1:10). We show Him our love by obeying His commands (John 14:23). He wants a broken and contrite heart and not a sacrifice or a list of good works (Psalm 51:16-17). We must have faith, believe that He is real, and by doing so, we will please Him (Hebrews 11:6).

PICK ONE OF THE VERSES FROM THIS LESSON AND WRITE IT BELOW.

DAY 2: STOP CONTROLLING OTHERS

Last week we talked about the illusion of control and that God is the only one who is really in control of situations and circumstances. In addition, there's one more area of control that is important to transforming our minds.

We need to stop trying to control others. We need to stop trying to make everyone like us. We need to curb our unrealistic expectations of others and celebrate their uniqueness.

The type of control we're going to look at today is control that exasperates others or causes strife and provokes quarrels. It's the kind of thinking that we are especially prone to when we first get married—or at least it was for me. I actually thought I could change my husband.

NAGGING, QUARRELSOME, PROVOKING

Controlling behavior can often be perceived by others as nagging, argumentative, quarrelsome, or provoking. Do you know someone who just loves to push your buttons to get a rise out of you? What about someone who tries to start arguments or even debates? Do you remind your spouse many times to do something? Those are just a few examples of behavior that can be a sign of trying to control others.

Read Proverbs 27:15-16. What image does it paint of someone who nags or is quarrelsome?

When we drone on and on to others around us, the sound of our voice becomes as annoying as a leaking roof or dripping faucet. People want to run away from us or hide out in the opposite corner of the house!

READ PROVERBS 19:13 FROM THE VERSIONS BELOW.

> A foolish child is a calamity to a father; a quarrelsome wife is as annoying as constant dripping. (NLT)

> A foolish child is a father's ruin, and a quarrelsome wife is like the constant dripping of a leaky roof. (NIV)

> A parent is worn to a frazzle by a stupid child; a nagging spouse is a leaky faucet. (The Message)

PROVERBS 19:13 TALKS ABOUT THREE PEOPLE: CHILD, PARENT, AND SPOUSE. WHAT BEHAVIOR IS MENTIONED SPECIFICALLY ABOUT THE CHILD AND SPOUSE? HOW DOES IT AFFECT OTHERS AROUND THEM?

CHILD –

WIFE/SPOUSE –

Our behavior affects those around us. When we nag, quarrel, or pick a fight with others, they can become frustrated, exasperated, angry, or frazzled. When we act foolishly we can bring more trouble upon those around us or even ourselves.

So, what can we do to combat this type of behavior in ourselves?

1. Deal with our negative thoughts that might be the root of our compulsion to nag.

2. Try asking questions when it comes to reminding someone to do something. For example, instead of saying "Don't forget to pick up the dry cleaning" you could ask, "Were you planning to pick up the dry cleaning today?"

3. Point out the good in others. Sometimes I find myself being overly critical towards someone. When I catch myself doing this, I try to think about that person's good qualities before engaging them.

4. Smile. Sometimes we forget how our facial expressions or body language can change how our words are perceived. By smiling, we can communicate to others that we mean no offense by our words.

PERSONAL REFLECTION: CAN YOU THINK OF OTHER WAYS TO HELP COMBAT ANY QUARRELSOME, PROVOKING, OR NAGGING TENDENCIES YOU MIGHT HAVE? IF SO, JOT THEM DOWN HERE. CONSIDER SHARING THESE IDEAS WITH YOUR GROUP.

TOGETHER, BUT SEPARATE

My husband and I have this saying: We are together but separate. We are part of the same marriage and continue to grow together as one, yet we are still individuals with our own unique personalities, hobbies, skills, and interests. Sometimes we say this when we are busy with hobbies or life to remind us that we are still together.

The Bible talks about this same concept as it relates to the church body.

READ 1 CORINTHIANS 12:18-30 THEN ANSWER THE FOLLOWING QUESTIONS.

WHO ARE THE "PARTS IN THE BODY"? WHO IS "THE BODY"?

WHO PLACED THE PARTS OF THE BODY WHERE THEY ARE?

WHAT HAPPENS WHEN THE PARTS OF THE BODY ARE NOT WORKING TOGETHER (V25)?

WHAT DOES VERSE 26 SAY ABOUT HOW INTERCONNECTED WE ARE WITH OTHERS?

The list of church roles in verses 28-30 is not a complete list. There are many different roles in the church.

Although this passage is talking about the church, we can draw some parallels to a marriage, a family, or even a team at work. Everyone has a part in a marriage. Everyone has a part in a family. Everyone has a part on a team. Each part is important and significant.

WHAT DOES GENESIS 1:27 SAY?

That's right, we are created in God's image—every single one of us. Our belief in Him, or someone's lack of it, does not change that.

HOW DOES THINKING ABOUT OTHERS AS MADE IN THE IMAGE OF GOD CHANGE YOUR PERSPECTIVE ON YOUR RELATIONSHIPS?

WHO ACCEPTED US ACCORDING TO ROMANS 15:7?

WHAT SHOULD WE DO AS A RESULT?

IS THERE ANYONE THAT YOU NEED TO ADJUST YOUR THINKING ABOUT BASED ON WHAT YOU'VE LEARNED IN TODAY'S LESSON?

SPEAK LIFE

The singer, Toby Mac, has a song called "Speak Life" and the quotes he posts on Facebook are often encouraging us to do exactly that. Yet, Toby Mac didn't invent the idea.

READ EPHESIANS 4:29. WHAT DOES IT SAY ABOUT HOW WE SHOULD SPEAK TO OTHERS?

Some synonyms for "unwholesome" are: noxious, sickly, unhealthy, unsanitary, poisonous, toxic, fatal, lethal, degraded, demoralizing, perverse, warped, corrupt.[23]

WHAT DO YOU THINK "UNWHOLESOME TALK" MEANS?

I know that I have said unhealthy things in my life—unhealthy for me and unhealthy for those around me. I have demoralized others. I have even said some poisonous and toxic things.

As I learn to change how I think about other people, I am more aware of what I say to or about others.

So, we know that our thoughts affect the words we speak. Can our words affect our thoughts? I think so.

READ PSALM 19:14. WHAT DOES THIS SAY ABOUT WHAT WE SAY AND THINK?

READ THE FOLLOWING VERSES AND NOTE WHAT THEY SAY ABOUT THE WORDS WE SPEAK. ALSO, NOTE THE EFFECT OF THOSE WORDS.

PROVERBS 16:24

COLOSSIANS 4:6

1 THESSALONIANS 5:11

HEBREWS 3:13

---

[23] "unwholesome." *Merriam-Webster.com*. Merriam-Webster, 2011. Web. 4 Jun 2016.

When we speak with grace and encouragement, others are built up, not torn down. When we speak life, our words are sweet and healing to others and even to ourselves.

As you go about your day, remember how special each person is who crosses your path. Then think and speak life-giving words.

PERSONALIZE ONE VERSE FROM TODAY'S LESSON.

DAY 3: GET OUT OF THEIR MINDS

My husband is a very upright, honest, and trustworthy person. Yet, I used to never believe anything he said. It wasn't because of *his character*. It was because of *my thoughts*.

I assumed that the good things he was trying to say could not be true because I did not believe that I was a good person. I felt worthless inside and assumed that meant I was worthless. So, when my husband said things like what a great worker I was in my career or how I made a good meal, I picked apart everything he said.

My thinking clouded my ability to hear what he was really saying. I just needed to get out of his mind and stop assuming I knew what he was thinking!

ASSUMING

Merriam-Webster's dictionary defines "assume" as:

> To think that something is true or probably true without knowing that it is true.[24]

---

[24] "assume." *Merriam-Webster.com*. Merriam-Webster, 2011. Web. 4 Jun 2016.

That's exactly what I was doing with my husband. I was convinced that something other than the truth was really the truth without really knowing.

PERSONAL REFLECTION: CAN YOU THINK OF A TIME WHEN YOU GOT INTO TROUBLE OR A CONFLICT BECAUSE OF AN ASSUMPTION?

I also love the synonyms of "assume":

Guess	Conjecture	Presume
Speculate	Suppose	Surmise
Suspect	Suspicion	

DO ANY OF THESE SYNONYMS STAND OUT TO YOU? HOW DOES THIS HELP YOU UNDERSTAND WHEN YOU MIGHT BE ASSUMING SOMETHING?

WHAT DOES DEUTERONOMY 18:20 SAY RELATED TO PRESUMPTION?

Yikes. The presumptuous prophet is put to death! That's some dire consequences.

There is a story in the Bible about a rich man who makes some very incorrect assumptions and suffers great consequences.

The rich man assumed that he would live for a long time to come. He also assumed that his grain would not go bad. He assumed that there would be no issues with sitting back and relaxing. He assumed that his ground would yield abundant crops in the future when he was done making merry. He assumed his surplus was solely for his benefit.

The consequences of his assumptions were dire. God took his life that night because of his greed.

SELF-DECEPTION

A close cousin to assumption is self-deception. When we believe something that isn't true, we are deceiving ourselves.

READ THE FOLLOWING VERSES AND NOTE WHAT THEY SAY ABOUT SELF-DECEPTION.

ISAIAH 5:21

JEREMIAH 17:9

1 CORINTHIANS 3:18

We can very easily deceive ourselves without intending to. We can become blind to the truth if we don't examine our thoughts.

The context of this verse is about testing and examining our faith. In the same way, I think it is a good practice to test and examine our thoughts to ensure that we do not deceive ourselves.

READ JOHN 16:7-11. WHAT DOES THIS SAY ABOUT THE HOLY SPIRIT (ADVOCATE)?

DO YOU TRUST THAT THE HOLY SPIRIT CAN HELP YOU DISCERN WHETHER OR NOT YOU ARE DECEIVING YOURSELF? WHY OR WHY NOT?

The Holy Spirit helps us have discernment. He helps us test ourselves and our thoughts to understand what our true motivations are. He helps us change our thinking and move from a self-deceiving mindset.

Nonetheless, we can go back to that place of self-deception if we are not vigilant. We must make evaluating our thought lives a priority.

JUDGING

When we assume we know what other people are thinking, we are judging either them or their words and actions without really knowing the truth.

As I shared at the opening of today, I had a problem with this for many years in my marriage. Then I realized that I was judging my husband based entirely on a set of false beliefs developed out of my assumptions.

READ THE FOLLOWING VERSES AND NOTE WHAT THEY SAY ABOUT
JUDGING OTHERS.

MATTHEW 7:1-2

LUKE 6:37

JOHN 7:24

READ ROMANS 2:1-3. WHAT HAPPENS WHEN WE PASS JUDGMENT ON
OTHERS FOR THE SAME SINS WE OURSELVES COMMIT?

This passage in Romans is very convicting. I know how many times I gossiped at work. I know how many times I envied someone else— that person who got the promotion or the person whose life seemed so easy compared to mine. I know how many times I coveted a larger house or fancier car.

This passage in Romans tells me that I do not have a leg to stand on. Judgment is not my job. It is God's alone.

Judgment is God's job, not mine

PARANOIA

When our assumptions are left unchecked and are rooted in fear, we are in danger of becoming paranoid. I am not talking about clinical paranoia. Instead, I am talking about the kind that leaves us suspicious and skeptical of others when there is no basis for such thinking.

In 1 Chronicles 19, King David had good intentions. When Hanun's father, the Ammonite king, died David sent envoys to Hanun because of the kindness David had been shown by Hanun's father.

WHAT MOTIVATED HANUN'S RESPONSE?

Hanun was suspicious and paranoid. He listened to his advisors who convinced him that David was insincere, and that David had ulterior motives.

Because of Hanun's response, over time, David sent his army to attack Hanun's armies and allies. All of this because Hanun was suspicious!

BELIEVE THE BEST

Part of loving others means we move beyond our assumptions and practice believing the best instead of assuming the worst about others.

WHAT DOES 1 CORINTHIANS 13:5-7 SAY ABOUT LOVE?

Love protects. Love trusts. Love hopes. Love is kind. Love does not have a hidden agenda. Love believes the best.

WHICH DO YOU STRUGGLE WITH THE MOST: ASSUMPTION, JUDGING, SELF-DECEPTION, OR PARANOIA?

HOW HAS IT AFFECTED YOUR RELATIONSHIPS?

PRAY AND ASK THE SPIRIT TO SHOW YOU WHEN YOU ARE ASSUMING, DECEIVING YOURSELF, JUDGING, OR BELIEVING THE WORST. ASK HIM TO HELP YOU CHANGE COURSE THE NEXT TIME YOU DO THIS.

PICK ONE VERSE FROM TODAY'S LESSON AND PERSONALIZE IT BELOW.

DAY 4: TAKE OFF YOUR MASK

This week we are talking about relating to other people and how our thoughts influence those relationships. No discussion on this would be complete without studying a simple word packed full of meaning: integrity.

Merriam-Webster defines "integrity" as:

> The quality of being honest and fair. The state of being complete or whole. A firm adherence to a code of especially moral or artistic values. An unimpaired condition. The quality or state of being complete or undivided.[25]

Integrity means that we are who we say we are and we act the same whether in church, at Bible study, in our homes, at our jobs, and when we are with friends and family.

THE MASKS WE WEAR

Many years ago, I remember hearing a sermon about integrity. When I evaluated myself, I could not say confidently that I was the same

---

[25] "integrity." *Merriam-Webster.com*. Merriam-Webster, 2011. Web. 18 Jun 2016.

Karen Baney at church, at home, or at work. I was very inconsistent, and I wore masks to keep people from getting to know the real me.

At work, I wore the "dedicated hard-worker" mask. At home, I tried to wear the "perfect wife" mask, and more often ended up wearing the "I feel safe so I'm going to act how I want" mask. At church, I wore the "compassionate and knowledgeable facilitator" mask.

In reality, I felt different from any of those masks. I felt insecure, unworthy, and even hopeless.

When I speak about wearing masks, I'm not talking about healthy boundaries in relationships. It is perfectly acceptable and healthy to reserve parts of yourself for a safe close friend or spouse. Exposing our entire heart to everyone that we meet is not safe or healthy or following God's Word. We are to guard our hearts (Proverbs 4:23).

But, there is a difference between guarding our hearts and projecting a false image to those around us.

PERSONAL REFLECTION: TAKE SOME TIME TO PRAY. ASK THE HOLY SPIRIT TO REVEAL TO YOU ANY MASKS THAT YOU HAVE EITHER WORN IN THE PAST OR ARE WEARING NOW. WRITE DOWN WHAT YOU HEAR FROM HIM.

DOUBLE-MINDED

Being double-minded is the opposite of integrity. Double-minded is one of the ways that the Bible describes a person who wears a mask and does not live with integrity.

GO BACK TO THE DEFINITION OF INTEGRITY ON THE FIRST PAGE OF TODAY'S LESSON. WRITE DOWN THE LAST SENTENCE OF THE DEFINITION IN THE SPACE BELOW.

When we are double-minded and wear masks, we are not complete or whole. Wholeness and completeness come when we are always the same person.

WHAT DOES PSALMS 62:4B SAY ABOUT THE DOUBLE-MINDED?

READ ISAIAH 29:13-16. HOW DOES GOD FEEL WHEN OUR WORDS AND ACTIONS DON'T LINE UP?

READ JEREMIAH 3:10. WHAT WORDS ARE USED TO DESCRIBE JUDAH?

The NIV uses the word "pretense" to describe a half-hearted attempt to return to God.

The double-minded person often interacts with others under a pretense. When we hide our true selves, we are giving an act or appearance that looks real but is false.

WHAT ADDITIONAL CHARACTERISTICS OF THE DOUBLE-MINDED DO WE FIND IN JAMES 1:5-8?

Remember from earlier in our study that we talked about our thoughts or heart being the source of our actions. Is it possible that our thoughts, our fears, our insecurity, or any number of other feelings could be the source of our double-mindedness?

UNDIVIDED HEART

The Bible also refers to double-mindedness as a divided heart.

WHAT DOES EZEKIEL 33:30-32 SAY ABOUT A DIVIDED HEART, ESPECIALLY IN THE PRACTICE OF OUR FAITH?

WHAT DOES MARK 7:6-8 CALL SOMEONE WHO HAS A DIVIDED HEART?

WHAT ELSE CAN WE LEARN FROM THIS PASSAGE ABOUT INSINCERE RELIGION?

When we have a divided heart in our relationship with God, we tend to move towards a more legalistic or rules-based religion full of human traditions. Our hearts remain at a distance.

HEART TRANSPLANT

To live with integrity, we need a heart transplant.

WHAT DOES PSALMS 86:11 SAY ABOUT HOW WE CAN HAVE AN UNDIVIDED HEART?

Jesus is our heart trans- plant

ACCORDING TO JEREMIAH 24:7, HOW CAN WE HAVE WHOLE HEARTS?

WHAT IS THE PRIMARY INGREDIENT TO BECOMING NEW ACCORDING TO 2 CORINTHIANS 5:17?

When we turn to God, He makes our hearts new, undivided, and whole. With Christ in us, we are new. All the old ways of thinking and behaving are gone! He is our heart transplant—another step towards our transformation with renewed minds.

PERSONALIZE ONE VERSE FROM THIS LESSON IN THE SPACE BELOW.

DAY 5: CONFLICT RESOLUTION

When it comes to learning to love one another, we will inevitably be confronted with conflict. We get along easily with those who are easy to love. Those that are hard to love—well, loving them will probably involve some conflict.

For me, conflict used to be a dirty word. I feared conflict. I avoided conflict. I ran from conflict.

Then I learned that there were some very Biblical ways to deal with conflict that were much better for both me and the other party(ies) involved in the conflict.

READ PHILIPPIANS 2:1-8. WHAT MINDSET SHOULD WE EXHIBIT (V2)?

WHAT KIND OF ATTITUDE APPEARS IN VERSE 3?

WHAT HAPPENS WHEN WE PUT THE INTERESTS OF OTHERS BEFORE OUR OWN INTERESTS?

WHAT ATTITUDE DID CHRIST EXHIBIT IN VERSES 5-8?

HOW CAN WE APPLY THIS PASSAGE TO THE CONFLICT WE HAVE WITH OTHERS?

Today, we're going to study five Biblical principles we can use to help deal with conflict in our lives.

1. Keep the conflict private
2. Deal with it quickly
3. Forgive
4. Speak truth in love
5. Be a peacemaker during times of conflict

KEEP CONFLICT PRIVATE

One of the fastest ways to escalate conflict and damage relationships is by gossiping. Gossiping can take several forms. Whether you talk bad about that person to your spouse, or you type out little jabs against that person on social media, you are breaking a confidence and adding fuel to the fire.

HOW DOES MATTHEW 18:15-17 SUGGEST WE HANDLE CONFLICT?

If necessary, Matthew 18:16 suggests we use a mediator. Otherwise, we are better off dealing with the conflict privately and directly with the person whom we had the conflict.

WHAT DOES JAMES 5:16 TELL US ABOUT THE ROLE OF PRAYER IN DEALING WITH SIN OR CONFLICT?

DEAL WITH IT QUICKLY

What happens when we run from conflict or delay dealing with it? The conflict does not go away on its own. Nor does it get better, unless it was over something that I needed to change in me. Usually, if we do not deal with conflict it gets worse.

WHAT HAPPENS ACCORDING TO EPHESIANS 4:26-27 WHEN WE DO NOT DEAL WITH OUR ANGER QUICKLY?

HOW DOES JESUS TELL US TO DEAL WITH CONFLICT IN MATTHEW 5:23-26?

We are to stop what we are doing and immediately go deal with the conflict.

WHY DO YOU THINK THIS IS SO HARD FOR US TO DO?

WHAT DOES VERSE 15 SAY ABOUT A BITTER ROOT?

When we do not deal with conflict quickly, it becomes bitter. The longer it is left unattended, the deeper it grows—turning into a bitter root. Then the bitter root (or bitterness and anger) causes trouble and defiles us and others.

Conflict that is dealt with quickly gives no opportunity for bitterness and anger to fester in our hearts and minds.

FORGIVE

Not forgiving someone is like drinking poison and expecting the other person to die. –Unknown

Forgiveness is not easy. When we forgive, we are not saying that what the other person did was okay. Instead, we choose to move past the offense.

READ EPHESIANS 4:31-32. WHAT IS THE CONNECTION BETWEEN BITTER-NESS AND FORGIVENESS?

Bitterness keeps us from being able to forgive others like Christ forgave us.

READ COLOSSIANS 3:12-14. WHAT ARE WE TO CLOTHE OURSELVES WITH ACCORDING TO VERSE 12?

VERSE 13 IS SANDWICHED BETWEEN THE LIST OF GOOD VIRTUES AND THE VERSE ABOUT PUTTING ON LOVE. WHY DO YOU THINK THE APOSTLE PAUL TALKS ABOUT FORGIVENESS IN THIS CONTEXT?

I think Paul tossed forgiveness and bearing with one another in the middle of these great virtues because without forgiveness it would be impossible for us to exhibit these virtues.

Before we finish this topic, there's one human nature trait that I want to address: revenge. It's ugly and it can sneak up on us when we least expect it.

Now you may be thinking to yourself at this point that you do not seek revenge and you are not out to hurt the person who offended you. Even so, have you ever been happy when that person gets their due? I have.

READ PROVERBS 24:17-18. WHAT HAPPENS WHEN WE REJOICE IN THE MISFORTUNE OF OUR ENEMIES?

Ouch! That's a tough passage to read. If we learn not to rejoice in our enemies' suffering, we will be better off.

PERSONAL REFLECTION: TAKE A MINUTE TO THINK ABOUT ANYONE YOU MIGHT FEEL BITTERNESS TOWARDS. HAVE YOU HELD ON TO AN OFFENSE OR CONFLICT? HAVE YOU PICKED UP AN OLD HURT AGAINST SOMEONE AND STARTED NURSING IT AGAIN? PRAY AND ASK GOD TO HELP YOU FORGIVE WHOEVER HE PUTS ON YOUR HEART.

TRUTH IN LOVE

Another aspect of dealing with conflict is how we speak to the person who offended us.

WHAT CAN WE LEARN FROM THE FOLLOWING VERSES ABOUT HOW WE SHOULD SPEAK TO THE PERSON WHO OFFENDED US?

PROVERBS 15:1

PROVERBS 21:23

EPHESIANS 4:15-16

COLOSSIANS 4:6

WHAT DO YOU THINK IT MEANS TO "SPEAK TRUTH IN LOVE"?

When we deal with conflict, we also need to take time to listen to the other person. Chances are they have some feelings they need to express to you.

WHAT CAN WE LEARN ABOUT LISTENING FROM JAMES 1:19-21?

WHAT DOES PROVERBS 18:13 TELL US?

To effectively deal with conflict, we need to let go of our anger and be cautious about what we say and when we say it. Sometimes this means stepping away from the conflict when it is heated so we can think calmly and deal with it in a godly way. So, there is a balance between dealing with conflict quickly and taking some time to cool down.

BE A PEACEMAKER

The last ingredient in dealing with conflict is being a peacemaker.

WHAT DO WE LEARN FROM THE FOLLOWING VERSES?

PSALM 34:14

ROMANS 12:18-19

TITUS 3:1-2

PERSONAL REFLECTION: DO YOU HAVE SOME UNRESOLVED CONFLICT IN A RELATIONSHIP? IF SO, WHICH ONE OF THE FIVE PRINCIPLES APPLIES TO THAT SITUATION? IF NOT, HOW CAN YOU APPLY THESE PRINCIPLES THE NEXT TIME YOU FACE CONFLICT?

PERSONALIZE ONE VERSE FROM TODAY'S LESSON.

Finally, brothers and sisters, whatever is true, whatever is noble, whatever is right, whatever is pure, whatever is lovely, whatever is admirable—if anything is excellent or praiseworthy—think about such things. –Philippians 4:8 (NIV)

NEW THOUGHTS

Ask yourself:

- Is this thought <u>true</u>? Is it _____ in _____

  and not disguised in a half-truth, deception, or lies?

- Is this thought <u>noble</u>? Is it _____ and

  _____ or worth thinking?

- Is this thought <u>right</u> or <u>righteous</u>? Is it _____ and

  _____?

- Is this thought <u>pure</u>? Does it show _____ for

  God and His _____?

- Is this thought <u>lovely</u>? Is it _____ and

  _____?

- Is this thought <u>admirable</u>? Does it deserve _____?

- Is this thought <u>excellent</u> or <u>praiseworthy</u>? Does it reveal an

  _____ of _____?

(continued on the next page)

POWER THOUGHTS

A "power thought" is a _____-_____ sentence

worded as an _____ and based on the

_____ of Scripture or _____

from God through Bible studies, books, prayer, wise counsel, or

journaling.

Example from Proverbs 29:25-26:

- I will not fear _____ but I will _____ and

  _____ only God.

- I will not seek _____. Instead, I will

  _____ God for _____.

Proverbs 3:5-6:

- I will do my _____ and leave the rest to _____.

Why craft power thoughts?

1. Easier to remember because they are personal.

2. Relevant to specific things I am dealing with.

3. Help me remember what God is teaching me.

FRESH START

Psalm 32 from The Message

_____

_____

_____

As we start our last week of study together, I want to congratulate you on persevering. We have covered a lot of topics related to our thoughts. I know this wasn't easy—but then the things that are the most worthwhile in life rarely are.

This week we are going to dive deeper into Philippians 4:8. We will wrap up with a day focused on writing out some Power Thoughts based on things you highlighted or starred or marked from this study. This is a very important part of the journey.

DAY 1: TRUE AND RIGHT

Then you will know the truth, and the truth will set you free. –John 8:32

I did not realize how very true John 8:32 was until I started asking if my thoughts were aligned with the truth. It is very humbling to learn that the thought patterns I have lived with for so long were frequently rooted in misperception or deception. It is not as if I was trying to deceive myself. It just happened. Or perhaps it was the enemy.

The truth exposes our thoughts and sets us free

Regardless, when our thoughts are exposed by the truth, the truth really does set us free.

GOD'S WORD IS TRUE

WHAT DOES PSALM 119:160 SAY ABOUT GOD'S WORD?

WHAT ELSE DO WE LEARN ABOUT THE TRUTH OF GOD'S WORD FROM JOHN 17:17?

The word "sanctification" in the NIV means the process of becoming holy. Sometimes we refer to this process as our walk or journey. It is a life-long process that, when we allow the Holy Spirit to work in us, he makes us more like Christ and like the person God made us to be.

READ EPHESIANS 1:13-14. WHAT IS THE MESSAGE OF TRUTH?

WHAT ELSE DO WE LEARN ABOUT OUR SALVATION FROM THESE VERSES?

GUIDED IN TRUTH

From Ephesians 1:13-14, we learn that when we became saved, the Holy Spirit began dwelling in us. He guides us and helps reveal the truth to us through scripture, prayer, wise counsel, and many other ways.

IN PSALM 25:5, WHERE DOES THE PSALMIST LOOK FOR GUIDANCE?

TOWARDS THE END OF THE VERSE, THE PSALMIST TALKS ABOUT HOPE. DO YOU THINK THERE IS A CONNECTION BETWEEN TRUTH AND HOPE? WHY OR WHY NOT?

IN PSALM 43:3, WHAT LEADS US AND WHERE DOES IT LEAD US?

When we seek the truth, we will find it and it will lead us to the very throne of God.

WHO IS TRUTH?

Is it possible that truth is a person?

READ JOHN 14:6. WHAT DOES JESUS SAY HE IS?

WHAT IS HE THE GATEKEEPER OF?

WHAT DOES JOHN 1:17 SAY ABOUT JESUS?

TRUTH IN OUR HEARTS

I once heard someone say that the truth is still the truth even if you don't believe it. As the Holy Spirit begins bringing our negative thoughts into our view, He also begins revealing the truth about those thoughts, even if we might not believe it.

For example, I used to believe that I hated asparagus. I thought it was gross and bitter. Then, one day I had grilled asparagus. It was amazing! The truth was not that I hated asparagus. I just hated asparagus from a can. If it is prepared on the grill or roasted in the oven, I love it.

In my life, I have clung to many false beliefs. Once I understood the truth, I became free.

IN JOSHUA 23, HE SUMMONS ISRAEL AND GIVES THEM ENCOURAGEMENT AND INSTRUCTION AT THE END OF HIS LIFE. READ JOSHUA 23:14. WHAT DOES HE SAY ABOUT THEIR HEART AND SOUL?

WHAT DOES HEBREWS 10:16 SAY THAT GOD PUTS IN OUR HEARTS AND MINDS?

We can know the truth. It is written on our hearts and in our minds. It is the Holy Spirit that reveals the truth to us.

THINK ABOUT IT

PERSONAL REFLECTION: ASK THE SPIRIT TO SHOW YOU AREAS OF YOUR LIFE WHERE YOU BELIEVE SOMETHING THAT ISN'T TRUE. HOW IS IT AFFECTING YOUR THOUGHTS? WHAT IS THE TRUTH?

RIGHT THINKING

What does Paul mean in Philippians 4:8 when he talks about "right" or "righteous" thinking? Some translations also use the word "just". Right thinking is when we focus on thoughts that are just and fair.

READ PROVERBS 12:5. WHAT DOES IT SAY ABOUT THE RIGHTEOUS?

WHAT MORE DO WE LEARN FROM PROVERBS 15:28 ABOUT THE HEART OF THE RIGHTEOUS?

Both verses from Proverbs paint a picture of being thoughtful, careful, and fair with what we say and think. That's what "right" thinking is.

WHAT IS "RIGHT" THINKING? WHAT IS ONE WAY YOU CAN FOCUS ON "RIGHT" THINKING?

PERSONALIZE ONE VERSE FROM TODAY'S LESSON.

DAY 2: NOBLE AND ADMIRABLE

Noble and admirable. These two words seem to go together well, even though they are not listed side by side in Philippians 4:8. A form of "admirable" is even used to define the word "noble".

> *Noble means: having, showing or coming from personal qualities that people admire (such as honesty, generosity, courage, etc.)*[26]

IN THE ABOVE DEFINITION OF NOBLE, UNDERLINE "PERSONAL QUALITIES" AND "ADMIRE." CAN YOU THINK OF ANOTHER WORD FOR "PERSONAL QUALITIES"? (HINT: READ RUTH 3:11)

FROM THE DEFINITION, WHAT ARE SOME OTHER ASPECTS OF NOBLE CHARACTER?

---

[26] "noble." *Merriam-Webster.com*. Merriam-Webster, 2011. Web. 24 Apr 2016.

Some synonyms for the word noble include:

Blameless	Honest	Decent
Gallant	Classy	Conscientious
Fair	Good	Incorruptible
Heroic	Honorable	Inspiring

If a thought is blameless or honest or decent or good, then it is a noble thought. If it inspires us, it is noble. If it is fair and honorable, then it is noble.

READ PSALM 15:1-5. WHERE CAN THE BLAMELESS LIVE?

WHAT ARE SOME OTHER CHARACTERISTICS OF THE BLAMELESS ACCORDING TO VERSES 2-5?

I also think there are three areas of our lives that we can examine to help us focus more on noble thoughts:

1. **What are we listening to?** This could be music, advice, audio books, etc. If we listen to words that encourage us or inspire us, then we tend to think about noble things.
2. **What are we seeing?** This could be TV shows, movies, images on the computer, Facebook, Instagram, etc. What we see with our eyes affects our thoughts.
3. **What is the source of what we believe?** Do we believe what our culture tells us? Or do our beliefs come from the Word of God?

Most recently, I have been thinking about what I see. I just finished binge watching one of my favorite TV shows yesterday. It is a spy thriller that is not something suitable for younger audiences. I love the show because it is full of intrigue.

Yet, when I woke up this morning, I felt out of sorts. A little grumpy and edgy. When I really considered where my feelings were coming from, I realized that I had watched way too much of that show yesterday (I think it was 5 episodes in one day). Watching too much was not good for me and it negatively influenced me.

I am not saying that we must only listen to Christian music or read Christian books or watch Christian TV shows. Rather, I am saying that all these things can influence our thoughts and make it more difficult to think noble thoughts.

PERSONAL REFLECTION: IS THERE SOMETHING IN YOUR LIFE THAT YOU ARE LISTENING TO, WATCHING, OR BELIEVING THAT IS MAKING IT HARDER TO THINK NOBLE THOUGHTS? IF SO, TAKE A MINUTE TO PRAY ABOUT IT. ASK THE SPIRIT TO SHOW YOU WHERE TO CHANGE.

ADMIRABLE

When someone is admirable, they are worthy of respect. Others want to be like them.

WHAT KIND OF THOUGHTS ARE DESERVING OF RESPECT?

WHO SHOULD WE IMITATE ACCORDING TO 1 CORINTHIANS 11:1?

In Philippians 2:5, Paul tells them to "have the same mindset as Christ Jesus."

READ PHILIPPIANS 2:1-11 AND MAKE NOTE OF EVERYTHING THE MINDSET OF CHRIST ENTAILS.

If we want to have admirable thoughts, our best example is imitating the mindset and thoughts of Christ.

HOW CAN YOU APPLY THIS PASSAGE TO YOUR LIFE?

PICK A VERSE FROM TODAY'S LESSON AND PERSONALIZE IT.

LOVELY

There are two places that I have visited in my life where not even a photograph can accurately portray the beauty: The Alps and the Grand Canyon.

The first time I visited the German side of the Alps was in late 1996. I was living in Germany at the time and a group of us were headed down to the southern end of the country to go on a skiing trip. I can still remember parts of the drive.

We were on a plateau and could see for miles around. Then the road dipped down. As we wound through switchbacks guarded by tall pines, we eventually came to the valley floor. Flat and grassy.

Then there they were. I started looking up and up and up. The tallest mountains I had ever seen stood there in great majesty, topped with snow covered peaks. No picture could ever fully capture the ethereal sense that comes from being so close to such towering mountains.

The second place that is almost too beautiful to convey is the Grand Canyon. Since I live in Arizona, I have visited the Grand Canyon many times. But, nothing will ever compare to the very first time.

I remember walking up to the edge—well, a good twenty feet or so back from the edge—and trying to take in the massiveness of the canyon. Purples, reds, and oranges streaked the craggy walls of the canyon. The deepest part of the canyon grew hazy and turned a shade of dark blue. As far as I could look to the east or the west, there were cliffs with unique jagged sides all pointing down, down, down to the valley floor before me. At some points along the rim, I could even see what I thought might be the river.

A deep breath to calm my nerves. Silence. Expanse. Color. There are not enough words to describe the scene before me.

Both the Alps and the Grand Canyon are examples of how lovely nature can be. One of the reasons I love exploring the state of Arizona is because of the amazing variety of landscapes and vistas, horizons and valleys. I never get tired of looking at it.

Another thing I find lovely are airplanes—especially those from WWII. On my home office walls, I have many WWII airplane photos I took from visiting several airplane museums in Arizona and California. It inspires my sense of awe in the ingenuity of man.

WHAT ARE SOME THINGS THAT YOU FIND LOVELY? HOW DO YOU FEEL WHEN YOU THINK ABOUT THEM?

There are so many lovely things to think about, like: nature, art, animals, children, architecture, etc.

Have you ever thought about how lovely God is or what He looks like? A few years ago, I dug through the Bible to see what it says about what God looks like, and the poem below was a result of what I found.

Glimpses of God by Karen Baney[27]

What do you look like?
Dare we even ask?
Shrouded in a dense cloud,
Your glory blazes like an all-consuming fire.
Your presence overwhelms,
Instilling near-death and trembling.
You are too awesome and powerful
For our minds to grasp.
Your throne is made of lapis lazuli,
Deep blue as the wide Arizona sky.
An emerald rainbow encircles your throne.
Fire, lightening, and thunder rumble from it.
The train of your robe fills the temple.
A sea of glass, clear as crystal,
Reflects the brilliance of your glory.
Your voice is like the multitude,
Loud like the rushing waters of tumultuous rapids.
When you speak, all creatures on heaven
And on earth fall at your feet.
Your power is like rays of the sun

---

[27] Inspired by: Ex. 24:10, Ex. 24:11, Ex. 24:16-17, Isaiah 6:1-8, Ezekiel 1:26-28, Daniel 7:9-11, Habakkuk 3:4, Rev. 1: 12-16, Rev. 4:2:6

Shooting out from your hands.
Though Your power is unparalleled,
So is Your infinite love.
You invite us into your presence
And let us dine with you.
You gave us a glimpse of yourself
By making us in your image.
You gave us all of yourself
Through the blood of your Son.
Let these thoughts motivate us
Spur us on to worship and love.
We are forever grateful,
To You, our Lord and God above.

WHAT ARE SOME THINGS THAT STOOD OUT TO YOU FROM THE POEM?

EXCELLENT

In our performance-driven society, it is easy to think of something excellent as being superior. If we see excellence as superiority, then the only excellent thing on which to think would be God himself.

However, excellence can be more than that. Excellence can mean something is exceptionally good or high quality. It can also mean something admirable or noble.

WHAT ARE SOME EXCELLENT THINGS YOU CAN THINK ABOUT?

PRAISEWORTHY

When something is praiseworthy, it is worthy of praise. Here are some synonyms for praiseworthy[28]:

Applaudable   Commendable   Deserving

Noteworthy   Precious   Valuable

Priceless

CERTAINLY, THE MOST PRAISEWORTHY BEING IS GOD. WHAT ELSE IS PRAISEWORTHY, NOTEWORTHY, PRECIOUS, OR VALUABLE?

VALUABLE TO GOD

Valuable is one of the synonyms of praiseworthy. This had me wondering what God might consider valuable. Surely, those would be good things to think about, right?

READ MATTHEW 12:9-13. WHAT DOES JESUS SAY IS VALUABLE IN VERSE 12?

People are valuable to God and helping people is important to Him.

READ JAMES 2:14-17. WHAT ROLE DO GOOD DEEDS PLAY IN OUR FAITH?

---

[28] "praiseworthy." *Merriam-Webster.com*. Merriam-Webster, 2011. Web. 24 Apr 2016.

WHAT HAPPENS IF WE ONLY HAVE FAITH WITHOUT ACTION TO BACK IT
UP?

Active faith is valuable to God.

READ THE FOLLOWING VERSES AND NOTE WHAT TYPES OF PEOPLE ARE
VALUABLE TO GOD.

DEUTERONOMY 14:28-29

ISAIAH 10:1-3

MATTHEW 6:1-4

JAMES 1:27

Active faith is valuable to God

When we think about widows, orphans, foreigners, the poor,
oppressed, and needy, then we are thinking about things that are
valuable to God. As we learned in James 2:14-17, when we actively
help these people, we are putting our faith into action.

Have you ever tried to help someone else when you feel down or
discouraged? If not, I would encourage you to do so. It can be a very
uplifting experience and even bring some perspective to your life.

GRATITUDE

Part of thinking about praiseworthy things involves exercising an
attitude of gratitude.

READ COLOSSIANS 3:15. WHAT IS TO RULE IN OUR HEARTS?

WHAT IS THE LAST SENTENCE OF COLOSSIANS 3:15?

HOW WOULD YOU DESCRIBE THE CONNECTION BETWEEN THANKFULNESS AND PEACE?

ACCORDING TO PSALM 69:30 AND PSALM 100:4, WHO DESERVES OUR PRAISE?

WHAT ACCOMPANIES PRAISE?

READ PSALM 95:2, 147:7, AND HEBREWS 12:28. WHEN WE ARE THANKFUL, WHAT ARE WE REALLY DOING?

When we tell God that we are thankful, we are worshipping and praising Him. Gratitude brings peace and helps us regain perspective. It brings honor and glory to God.

> *Gratitude is a cure for our bad moods and attitudes*

There's an old hymn that talks about counting your blessings. The songwriter reminds us that the time to count our blessings is when life is a wreck—when we're discouraged, burdened, facing conflict, or when we think all is lost.

The songwriter understood this truth about gratitude: Gratitude is a cure for our bad moods and attitudes.

MAKE A LIST OF FIVE THINGS YOU ARE THANKFUL FOR.

DAY 4: PURE

Finally, brothers and sisters, whatever is true, whatever is noble, whatever is right, whatever is pure, whatever is lovely, whatever is admirable—if anything is excellent or praiseworthy—think about such things. –Philippians 4:8

So far, we've talked about true, right, noble, admirable, lovely, excellent, and praiseworthy thoughts. I saved pure thoughts for last because there are a lot of aspects to pure thoughts.

WHAT IS PURE

When a precious metal, such as gold, is pure, it means that there are no traces of other substances and pollutants in it. In music, something pure has a smooth and clear sound. In sports, a pure shooter is someone who has the exact skills needed.

When something is pure we think of it as clean, decent, or morally acceptable. We know Jesus was without sin and therefore, He lived a pure life. We sing songs about how He cleans us whiter than snow and makes us pure.

READ PSALM 19:9. WHAT DOES THIS VERSE SAY IS PURE?

Wow. True purity is the fear and respect of God.

PURE IN HEART

READ MATTHEW 5:8 AND WRITE IT IN THE SPACE BELOW.

MATTHEW 5:8 REFERENCES PSALM 24:3-4. WHAT DO YOU THINK IT MEANS TO HAVE CLEAN HANDS AND A PURE HEART?

I find it interesting that in Psalm 24:4, that the definition of someone who has clean hands and a pure heart is someone who does not trust in idols or swear by a false god. The pure in heart is someone who allows God to work in them and root out the sin in their life.

HOW DOES 2 TIMOTHY 2:22 FURTHER OUR UNDERSTANDING OF THE PURE IN HEART?

The pure in heart are not perfect people. The pure in heart still sin. However, the pure in heart also deal with their stuff and seek God's Will.

When we do these things, we see God. We see Him actively changing our hearts and healing our hurts. We see Him clearing a path before us. We see evidence of His work all around us.

By participating in this study, if you are partnering with God and letting Him change you from the inside out, then you are the pure in heart.

GRACIOUS WORDS

One of the characteristics of the pure in heart is gracious words.

Did you catch the reference to thoughts in this verse? Gracious words don't just have to be the words we speak. They can also be the words we think. So, if we want to think on things that are pure—gracious words deserve some of our thought-focus.

What are some gracious words you can think or say related to a difficult situation or person in your life?

PURITY WITH OUR BODIES

When we look for verses in the Bible that talk about pure thoughts or purity, we will find many verses that talk about sexual purity and sexual immorality.

I'll be honest. I really did not want to talk about this subject. Then again, our culture is filled with perverted images and words about this subject.

If you stop and think about the music on the top 40 charts or the most popular TV shows or the movies in the theaters this very moment, I am sure it will not take you long to find examples of ideas about sex and marriage that contradict God's Word.

Read Hebrews 13:4. What does it say should be kept pure?

In what ways do you feel our culture promotes the opposite of this?

WHY IS THAT SO IMPORTANT?

WHERE DOES MATTHEW 5:28 SAY LUST BEGINS?

Our lustful or sexually impure actions flow from our thoughts.

That means if we are fantasizing about someone other than our spouse, if we are thinking too often about that co-worker, if we reason away looking at pornography, or anything that falls under the sexually immoral category, then we are in danger of acting on those thoughts.

And, as we learned from 1 Corinthians 6:18, acting on sexually impure thoughts is the most damaging sin to ourselves.

When it comes to sexual thoughts that are pure, let me clear up a misunderstanding. Pure thoughts are not necessarily prudish thoughts. In marriage, you can still be attracted to your spouse and act on that attraction. You can still think about your spouse in a sexual way. Sexual purity can involve an active and satisfying sexual relationship with your spouse.

The best offense for remaining sexually pure in our lives, regardless of our marital status, is by thinking pure thoughts.

PERSONAL REFLECTION: ASK THE HOLY SPIRIT TO SHOW YOU ANY AREAS OF YOUR THOUGHT LIFE THAT ARE NOT SEXUALLY PURE. PRAY AND ASK HIM TO HELP YOU CHANGE YOUR THINKING.

DAY 5: PERSONALIZED POWER THOUGHTS

You made it. Today is your last day of personal study. I hope the journey has changed you. I hope you have grown closer to God and understand how our thoughts impact so many different areas of our lives.

I also hope you have experienced some healing for harmful thought patterns.

LASTING CHANGE

I recently wrote this thought in my journal:

Lasting growth is born from pain that is covered by mercy.

From personal experience, I know that changing your thinking is hard and downright painful at times. The journey would not be possible without God's mercy.

I want to focus our time today on taking some steps to help us remember the things we learned in this study.

Lasting growth is born from pain that is covered by mercy

PERSONALIZED POWER THOUGHTS

In session six, I talked about power thoughts. I defined a power thought as a truth-filled sentence worded as an intention and based on the principles of scripture or revelation from God through Bible studies, books, prayer, wise counsel, or journaling.

Samples:

- I will do my best and leave the rest to God. (Proverbs 3:5-6)
- It is God who works in me to change my mind and thinking. I just need to trust him. (Isaiah 26:3)
- I will not compare myself to others; not for boosting my ego, nor for belittling myself. (Isaiah 2:22)
- God's truth is my foundation and I will seek to understand it. (Proverbs 2:1-6)
- I choose to put on a new positive attitude daily. (Ephesians 4:22-24)

I've included a list of almost fifty of my power thoughts in Appendix B as a reference as you write your own. You can use the following questions as a guide:

- What did I learn from this verse?
- How did God speak to me through this verse?
- What truth can I find about myself or God in this verse?
- What new thought pattern does this verse reinforce?
- What old thought pattern does this verse challenge?

Start with the verses you personalized at the end of each day in your homework. Also, look at anything you highlighted or marked from each lesson.

PERSONALIZED POWER THOUGHTS FROM WEEK 1

TAKE A FEW MINUTES TO CRAFT SOME PERSONALIZED POWER THOUGHTS
TO HELP YOU REMEMBER WHAT YOU LEARNED DURING WEEK 1.

CRAFT SOME PERSONALIZED POWER THOUGHTS FROM THE LESSONS OF WEEK 2.

CRAFT SOME PERSONALIZED POWER THOUGHTS FROM THE LESSONS OF WEEK 3.

CRAFT SOME PERSONALIZED POWER THOUGHTS FROM THE LESSONS OF WEEK 4.

CRAFT SOME PERSONALIZED POWER THOUGHTS FROM THE LESSONS OF WEEK 5.

CRAFT SOME PERSONALIZED POWER THOUGHTS FROM THE LESSONS OF
WEEK 6.

WHY CONTINUE THE JOURNEY?

LET'S READ ROMANS 12:2 ONE MORE TIME. ACCORDING TO THIS VERSE,
WHY DO WE STRIVE TO BE TRANSFORMED?

This entire study has been about being transformed by the renewing
of our minds. We do this, so we can know God's will and do God's
will. We do this with the Spirit's guidance and help.

Fix these words of mine in your hearts and minds; tie them as symbols on your hands and bind them on your foreheads.
–Deuteronomy 11:18

REMEMBER

The _____ will _____ us of what we've learned. (John 14:26)

Keep using God's Word as a _____ against

_____ thoughts. (Eph 6:14-17)

Put what you learn into _____ and keep

_____. (Phil. 4:9)

PRACTICAL STEPS TO REMEMBER

1. Take some time to go back and finish any homework you missed.
2. Add notes to your journal or keep this study book so you can refer to what you've learned, especially in the hard times.
3. Add the most helpful power thoughts to your phone so you can read them whenever you need a reminder.
4. Print out your power thoughts and fix them to your bathroom mirror
5. Evaluate your thoughts.

_____

_____

_____

_____

_____

_____

Search for Significance by Robert S. McGee

Unglued by Lysa TerKeurst

So Long, Insecurity by Beth Moore

Me, Myself, and Lies by Jennifer Rothschild (Bible Study)

Lessons I Learned in The Dark by Jennifer Rothschild

You're Already Amazing: Embracing Who You Are, Becoming All God Created You to Be by Holley Gerth

Anxious for Nothing: God's Cure for the Cares of Your Soul by John MacArthur

Anxious for Nothing: Finding Calm in a Chaotic World by Max Lucado

Breaking Busy: How to Find Peace and Purpose in a World of Crazy by Alli Worthington

Unstuck by Chip Ingram (Podcast series and book)

What Women Fear by Angie Smith

These are great resources for learning more about your personality:

Please Understand Me II by David Keirsey

Personality Plus by Florence Littauer

The power to live a changed life comes from God and the Holy Spirit. I need to choose daily to pursue Him.

> For the kingdom of God is not a matter of talk but of power. –1 Corinthians 4:20

God is in control, so I don't have to be.

> I form the light and create darkness, I bring prosperity and create disaster; I, the Lord, do all these things. –Isaiah 45:7

My ministry helping others at work and at church is seen by God and He sees my love for Him in it.

> God is not unjust; he will not forget your work and the love you have shown him as you have helped his people and continue to help them. –Hebrews 6:10

If I am discouraged as I am growing and changing my thinking, I will remember that healing comes through the journey.

> And as they went, they were cleansed. –Luke 17:14b

I will trust and fear God and not fear humans.

> Fear of man will prove to be a snare, but whoever trusts in the Lord is kept safe. –Proverbs 29:25

> Stop trusting in mere humans, who have but a breath in their nostrils. Why hold them in esteem? –Isaiah 2:22

> So we say with confidence, "The Lord is my helper; I will not be afraid. What can mere mortals do to me?" –Hebrews 13:6

I will not seek revenge, but instead I will trust God for justice.

> Many seek an audience with a ruler, but it is from the Lord that one gets justice. –Proverbs 29:26

God can use me for his kingdom purposes even when I am sick or dealing with chronic illnesses.

> As you know, it was because of an illness that I first preached the gospel to you, and even though my illness was a trial to you, you did not treat me with contempt or scorn.

> Instead, you welcomed me as if I were an angel of God, as if I were Christ Jesus himself. —Galatians 4:13-14

I can change my thinking with God's help and when I do so, I experience peace.

> You will keep in perfect peace those whose minds are steadfast, because they trust in you. —Isaiah 26:3

> And the peace of God, which transcends all understanding, will guard your hearts and minds in Christ Jesus. —Philippians 4:7

> We demolish arguments and every pretension that sets itself up against the knowledge of God, and we take captive every thought to make it obedient to Christ. —2 Corinthians 10:5

There is life in thinking positively.

> The mind governed by the flesh is death, but the mind governed by the Spirit is life and peace. —Romans 8:6

When someone offends me, I need to forgive them quickly.

> Make every effort to live in peace with everyone and to be holy; without holiness no one will see the Lord. —Hebrews 12:14

I will do my best and leave the rest to God.

> Trust in the Lord with all your heart and lean not on your own understanding; in all your ways submit to him, and he will make your paths straight. —Proverbs 3:5-6

No one can accuse me because I believe in Christ and his righteousness covers me.

> This is why "it was credited to him as righteousness." The words "it was credited to him" were written not for him alone, but also for us, to whom God will credit righteousness—for us who believe in him who raised Jesus our Lord from the dead. He was delivered over to death for our sins and was raised to life for our justification. —Romans 4:22-25

Perfectionism is an idol in my life and I need to confess it.

> All who make idols are nothing, and the things they treasure are worthless. Those who would speak up for them are blind; they are ignorant, to their own shame. Who shapes a god and casts an idol, which can profit nothing? –Isaiah 44:9-10

Comparing myself to others, whether to bolster my view of myself or to degrade it, is a sin.

> Stop trusting in mere humans, who have but a breath in their nostrils. Why hold them in esteem? –Isaiah 2:22

The Spirit's job is to carry the burden of making me righteous. Mine is to allow him.

> Therefore, get rid of all moral filth and the evil that is so prevalent and humbly accept the word planted in you, which can save you. Do not merely listen to the word, and so deceive yourselves. Do what it says. –James 1:21-22

God's truth is my foundation and I will seek to understand it.

> My son, if you accept my words and store up my commands within you, turning your ear to wisdom and applying your heart to understanding—indeed, if you call out for insight and cry aloud for understanding, and if you look for it as for silver and search for it as for hidden treasure, then you will understand the fear of the Lord and find the knowledge of God. For the Lord gives wisdom; from his mouth come knowledge and understanding.–Proverbs 2:1-6

I choose to put on a new attitude daily.

> You were taught, with regard to your former way of life, to put off your old self, which is being corrupted by its deceitful desires; to be made new in the attitude of your minds; and to put on the new self, created to be like God in true righteousness and holiness. –Ephesians 4:22-24

I choose to speak words of life that build up others.

> Do not let any unwholesome talk come out of your mouths, but only what is helpful for building others up according to their needs, that it may benefit those who listen. –Ephesians 4:29

I can learn anything I need to learn whether it is in business or life or faith.

> If any of you lacks wisdom, you should ask God, who gives generously to all without finding fault, and it will be given to you. –James 1:5

I will listen for God's truth and not follow what our culture says is true.

> Woe to those who call evil good and good evil, who put darkness for light and light for darkness, who put bitter for sweet and sweet for bitter. –Isaiah 5:20

I will trust and obey God. His vision goes far beyond mine.

> If people can't see what God is doing, they stumble all over themselves; But when they attend to what he reveals, they are most blessed. –Proverbs 29:18 (The Message)

I choose to persevere in the face of the many trials that come my way so that I may become complete.

> Consider it pure joy, my brothers and sisters, whenever you face trials of many kinds, because you know that the testing of your faith produces perseverance. Let perseverance finish its work so that you may be mature and complete, not lacking anything. –James 1:2-4

I am a daughter of the Most High King and I am created in His image.

> Then God said, "Let us make mankind in our image, in our likeness, so that they may rule over the fish in the sea and the birds in the sky, over the livestock and all the wild animals, and over all the creatures that move along the ground." So God created mankind in his own image, in the image of God he created them; male and female he created them. –Genesis 1:26-27

> Yet to all who did receive him, to those who believed in his name, he gave the right to become children of God. –John 1:12

I am called according to God's purpose and He's got this (whatever thing I am worried about).

And we know that in all things God works for the good of those who love him, who have been called according to his purpose. –Romans 8:28

I belong to You and You call me royal.

But you are a chosen people, a royal priesthood, a holy nation, God's special possession, that you may declare the praises of him who called you out of darkness into his wonderful light. –1 Peter 2:9

I am holy and blameless.

For he chose us in him before the creation of the world to be holy and blameless in his sight. –Ephesians 1:4

I have power, love, and self-control through the Spirit.

For the Spirit God gave us does not make us timid, but gives us power, love and self-discipline. –2 Timothy 1:7

God does not change, and he is the source of good things in my life.

Every good and perfect gift is from above, coming down from the Father of the heavenly lights, who does not change like shifting shadows. –James 1:17

I will do what God's word says and I will remember it.

Do not merely listen to the word, and so deceive yourselves. Do what it says. Anyone who listens to the word but does not do what it says is like someone who looks at his face in a mirror and, after looking at himself, goes away and immediately forgets what he looks like. But whoever looks intently into the perfect law that gives freedom, and continues in it—not forgetting what they have heard, but doing it—they will be blessed in what they do. —James 1:22-25

I am complete in Christ.

For in Christ all the fullness of the Deity lives in bodily form, and in Christ you have been brought to fullness.

–Colossians 2:9-10a

I am Christ's and I am His desire.

I belong to my beloved, and his desire is for me. —Song of Songs 7:10

God rests his favor on me.

May the favor of the Lord our God rest on us. —Psalm 90:17a

When I seek God, I will find him.

You will seek me and find me when you seek me with all of your heart. —Jeremiah 29:13

God is in control, so I don't have to be.

I form the light and create darkness, I bring prosperity and create disaster; I, the Lord, do all these things. —Isaiah 45:7

The power to live a changed life comes from God and the Holy Spirit. I need to choose daily to pursue Him.

For the kingdom of God is not a matter of talk but of power. —1 Corinthians 4:20

May the God of hope fill you with all joy and peace as you trust in him, so that you may overflow with hope by the power of the Holy Spirit. —Romans 15:13

God provides for all my needs and he is capable of meeting those needs.

The God who made the world and everything in it is the Lord of heaven and earth and does not live in temples built by human hands. And he is not served by human hands, as if he needed anything. Rather, he himself gives everyone life and breath and everything else. —Acts 17:24-25

God is my strength when I am weary of my health issues.

He gives strength to the weary and increases the power of the weak. —Isaiah 40:29

It is not my job to carry the burden of **how** things will work out for me or for others.

The Lord knows how to rescue the godly from trials and to keep the unrighteous under punishment until the day of judgment. —2 Peter 2:9 HCSB

For he knows how we are formed, he remembers that we are dust. –Psalm 103:14 NIV

When I am having a hard time balancing my passion to do something with God's timing, I will remember that God is waiting alongside me.

Yet the Lord longs to be gracious to you; therefore he will rise up to show you compassion. For the Lord is a God of justice. Blessed are all who wait for him! –Isaiah 30:18

The Lord waits... blessed are those who wait for Him. –Isaiah 30:18 ESV

God empowers me to do what he calls me to do, so I do not have to be afraid.

After I looked things over, I stood up and said to the nobles, the officials and the rest of the people, Don't be afraid of them. Remember the Lord, who is great and awesome, and fight for your families, your sons and your daughters, your wives and your homes. –Nehemiah 4:14

When I have more on my plate than I think I can handle, I will cast it away from me towards God.

Cast all your anxiety on him because he cares for you. –1 Peter 5:7

As I persevere in the calling God placed on my life, I will remember what He told me, and I will remember to fight the battle with both faith and a good conscience.

Timothy, my son, I am giving you this command in keeping with the prophecies once made about you, so that by recalling them you may fight the battle well, holding on to faith and a good conscience, which some have rejected and so have suffered shipwreck with regard to the faith. –1 Timothy: 18-19

I will remember and share what God has revealed to me.

The secret things belong to the Lord our God, but the things revealed belong to us and to our children forever, that we may follow all the words of this law. –Deuteronomy 29:29

The plan God is working out through me will become beautiful at just the right time.

He has made everything beautiful in its time. –Ecclesiastes 3:11a

When I lean into God, I am sheltered and I can find rest and peace.

Whoever dwells in the shelter of the Most High will rest in the shadow of the Almighty. –Psalm 91:1

God's plan is good and for our good.

For it is God who works in you to will and to act in order to fulfill his good purpose. –Philippians 2:13

And we know that in all things God works for the good of those who love him, who have been called according to his purpose. –Romans 8:28

This study is designed for **seven** meetings.

Each week the video broaches the overarching topic which will be covered in more detail during the homework. The questions starting with "personal reflection" are not intended for group discussion.

At the end of each day of homework, there is space to personalize one of the verses used in the lesson. This will be used during an exercise in Week 6 (see page 149).

Additional Resources

www.karenbaney.com/be-transformed

- Session Answers

Session 1

Before the Session

Pray for each member by name. Ask the Holy Spirit to speak to each of the members and to remove any obstacles that might keep them from coming to class.

Have name tags ready, to help everyone learn each other's names.

Ice Breaker

Share a time when a movie scene stuck in your mind. What movie was it? Why did you keep thinking about that scene?

Session

Turn to the title page. Read Romans 12:2 out loud together. Encourage the class to memorize this verse.

Read the introduction together on pages iii – iv.

Video

Play the video *Session 1: Mind Games*.

Discussion Questions

1.   What stood out to you the most from the

Introduction or Session 1? Why?

2.   How do you feel knowing that our thoughts matter to God?

3.   Were you surprised to learn that He made sure there were so many verses in the Bible about our mind, heart, and thoughts?

4.   How is the world's way of renewing our minds different from God's way?

5.   What do you hope to gain from this study?

Closing

Remind the class to mark or highlight anything that stands out to them as they go along in the study. We will be using those notes for an exercise during the last week of homework.

Pray that God would help each class member believe that their thoughts are important to Him and that he wants to help them learn healthy thought patterns.

Session 2

Before the Session

Pray for each member by name. Ask the Holy Spirit to speak to each of the members and to remove any obstacles that might keep them from coming to class.

Have name tags ready, to help everyone learn each other's names.

Ice Breaker

Share a time when you tried to give up a habit or start a new habit. What was it like? How long did it take you to become comfortable with the change?

Session

Turn to the title page. Read Romans 12:2 out loud together. Encourage the class to memorize this verse.

Go through the discussion questions below prior to playing the video.

Discussion Questions

1.   Do you believe you can change your

thought patterns? Why or why not?

2. What stood out to you the most from the exercise on pages 5 – 6?
3. On pages 12 – 13, we read the story of David and Bathsheba. Where did David's sin begin?
4. What could David have done differently to keep from committing adultery and then murder?
5. On page 14, read Ephesians 4:22-24. How is this passage like our theme verse of Romans 12:2? How is it different?
6. On pages 17 – 18, how does the Bible help us change our thought patterns?
7. According to Galatians 5:16, how do we keep from gratifying the desires of the flesh? (page 19)

Video

Play the video *Session 2: Building a Good Foundation.*

Video Discussion Questions (opt.)

1. What did Jesus say about trials in John 16:33?
2. How do we build our foundation on the rock?
3. Who helps us in our weakness? How does He do this?
4. Where does our identity come from? How can we learn more about that identity?

Closing

Remind the class to mark or highlight anything that stands out to them as they go along in the study. We will be using those notes for an exercise during the last week of homework.

Pray that God would show class members practical and tangible ways they can build their foundation on Him. Ask that the Spirit would remind them of their identity in Christ.

Session 3

Before the Session

Pray for each member by name. Ask the Holy Spirit to speak to each of the members and to remove any obstacles that might keep them from coming to class.

Have name tags ready, to help everyone learn each other's names.

Ice Breaker

Can you think of a time when someone played a prank on you or someone teased you about something you thought was real, only to find out later it wasn't?

Session

Turn to the title page. Read Romans 12:2 out loud together. Encourage the class to memorize this verse.

Go through the discussion questions below prior to playing the video.

Discussion Questions

1. I'm not _____ enough. Which one of the "not enough's" on pages 23 – 28 did you relate to? Why?
2. Why should we stop beating ourselves up? (pages 28 – 32)
3. Which do you struggle with the most: having high expectations of yourself or trying to live up to other people's expectations? What was the most helpful verse or verses on pages 33 – 36?
4. How can taking ownership help us stop blaming others? (pages 37 – 38)
5. What did David do in a time of despair according to 1 Samuel 30:2-3 and Psalm 18:6? (pages 40 – 41)

Video

Play the video *Session 3: Our Minds, The Flesh, and Satan.*

Video Discussion Questions (opt.)

1. What is "the flesh"?
2. How can we combat our flesh?
3. What is Satan's plan?
4. What are some of Satan's tactics?
5. What are some of our weapons against Satan?

Closing

Remind the class to mark or highlight anything that stands out to them as they go along in the study. We will be using those notes for an exercise during the last week of homework.

Pray for the member's continued commitment to changing their thought patterns. Ask that God would give them the strength to fight their enemies: the flesh and Satan. Ask the Spirit to remind them of what they are learning.

Session 4

Before the Session

Pray for each member by name. Ask the Holy Spirit to speak to each of the members and to remove any obstacles that might keep them from coming to class.

Have name tags ready, to help everyone learn each other's names.

Ice Breaker

What is one thing that you don't like about yourself? This could be a physical attribute or a habit or a personality quirk.

Session

Turn to the title page. Read Romans 12:2 out loud together. Encourage the class to memorize this verse.

Go through the discussion questions below prior to playing the video.

Discussion Questions

1. Where does our identity come from? How does knowing our true identity help us change what we think? (pages 47 – 51)
2. On page 53, what did we learn from 2 Corinthians 12:9 about our state when God's power is made perfect? What does God provide to sustain us?
3. How can legalism keep us from changing our thought patterns?
4. Do we have to fear failure, shame, disgrace or humiliation? Why or why not? (pages 55 – 56)
5. What is the difference between guilt and conviction? How can we respond to our false guilt? What is the purpose of conviction? (pages 56 – 60)
6. How do pride, selfish ambition, and fits of rage (anger) keep us from changing our thought patterns? How can we combat pride, selfish ambition, and anger? (pages 62 – 66)

7. What is the purpose of our emotions? Where do our emotions stem from? How can we control our emotions? (pages 66 – 70)

Video

Play the video *Session 4: Fear, Worry & Anxiety*.

Video Discussion Questions (opt.)

1. How are fear, worry, and anxiety connected?
2. What can we remember to help us with our fear?
3. What does worry accomplish?
4. What thoughts can we focus on to overcome our worry?
5. What can we do to alleviate our anxiety?

Closing

Remind the class to mark or highlight anything that stands out to them as they go along in the study. We will be using those notes for an exercise during the last week of homework.

Pray that the class will remember that God provides everything we need the next time they feel worried. Ask the Spirit to remind them to cast their anxiety on Him.

Session 5

Before the Session

Pray for each member by name. Ask the Holy Spirit to speak to each of the members and to remove any obstacles that might keep them from coming to class.

Have name tags ready, to help everyone learn each other's names.

Ice Breaker

Have you ever been afraid of or worried about something, only later to find out that it was no big deal? Share with the class.

Session

Turn to the title page. Read Romans 12:2 out loud together. Encourage the class to memorize this verse.

Go through the discussion questions below prior to playing the video.

Discussion Questions

1. How do we disguise our "what if" worries so they seem like a good thing? What can we do to overcome our "what if" worries? What characteristic of God helps us? (pages 75 – 78)
2. How do our "why's" trap us in negative thoughts? What can we do to suffer well? What characteristic of God helps us change how we view our trials? (pages 78 – 81)
3. What are some of the things we worry about? (pages 82 – 83)
4. What characteristic of God helps us when we worry? (page 84)
5. How can worrying about our past affect our thoughts? What characteristic of God can help us overcome our past? (pages 85 – 88)
6. What is the root cause of our need to control? What is the characteristic of God that can help us change our controlling behaviors and thoughts? (pages 89 – 93)

Video

Play the video *Session 5: Love One Another (& Yourself)*.

Video Discussion Questions (opt.)

1. How does loving ourselves too much affect our relationships?
2. What is the opposite of self-centeredness?
3. How does loving ourselves too little affect our relationships?
4. What are some lessons we learn from Matthew 25:14-30?
5. What kind of self-image do we have when we love ourselves just right?
6. How does a sober self-image help us change our thought patterns?

Closing

Remind the class to mark or highlight anything that stands out to them as they go along in the study. We will be using those notes for an exercise during the last week of homework.

Pray that God will help each person have a sober and grounded self-image—that those with low self-esteem will see themselves as God does and

that those with self-centered tendencies will learn humility.

Session 6

Before the Session

Pray for each member by name. Ask the Holy Spirit to speak to each of the members and to remove any obstacles that might keep them from coming to class.

Have name tags ready, to help everyone learn each other's names.

Ice Breaker

Think of a time when misunderstanding something that someone said got you into trouble. Share it with the class.

Session

Turn to the title page. Read Romans 12:2 out loud together. Encourage the class to memorize this verse.

Go through the discussion questions below prior to playing the video.

Discussion Questions

1. Do you have some victories you would like to share from pages 96 – 98?
2. What happens when we place too much emphasis on pleasing others or when we become addicted to the approval of others? (pages 99 – 103)
3. What verse(s) can help you change your people pleasing to God-pleasing? (pages 103 – 104)
4. What negative behaviors do we exhibit when we try to control others? How does that affect our relationships? What words and thoughts can help make our relationships better? (pages 105 – 110)
5. How do our thoughts and assumptions about others impact our relationships? Can we trust our own judgment at all times? What happens when we judge others or act suspiciously? How can we change these thought patterns? (pages 111 – 116)
6. What are some of the masks you wear? What can change those masks? (pages 117 – 121)
7. What are the five principles for conflict

resolution? How can we apply these to our relationships? (pages 121 – 128)

(pages 121 – 128)

Video

Play the video *Session 6: Think on These Things*.

Video Discussion Questions (opt.)

1. What are some questions we can ask to help us evaluate our thoughts using Philippians 4:4-9?
2. What is a power thought?
3. How can a power thought help us change our thought patterns?
4. What stood out to you the most from the reading of Psalm 32?

Closing

At the end of this week, there is an exercise to write out power thoughts based on the things the members have highlighted throughout the class.

Pray that God will help everyone align their thoughts with His. Ask Him to be the source of the power thoughts that they will write later this week.

Session 7

Before the Session

Pray for each member by name. Ask the Holy Spirit to speak to each of the members and to remove any obstacles that might keep them from coming to class.

Ice Breaker

Have you ever tried to memorize something word for word? Was it easy or hard? Why?

Session

Turn to the title page. Read Romans 12:2 out loud together.

Go through the discussion questions below prior to playing the video.

Discussion Questions

1. What is the purpose of truth? How does knowing the truth from Scripture help us change our thought patterns? (pages 133 –

135)
2. What is "right or righteous thinking"? How does "right thinking" help us change our thought patterns? (pages 136 – 137)
3. What are noble and admirable thoughts? What are three areas of our lives we can examine to see if our thoughts are noble and admirable? (pages 137 – 140)
4. What are some things that you find lovely that can help you change your thought patterns? (pages 141 – 143)
5. What is valuable to God? How is gratitude related to excellent and praiseworthy thoughts? (pages 145 – 146)
6. How does purity play a role in our thought patterns? What kind of words come from the pure in heart? (pages 147 – 151)
7. Spend some time sharing personalized power thoughts. (pages 151 – 158)
8. Why should we continue to learn even after this study is done? (page 158)

Video

Play the video *Session 7: The Transformation Process*.

Video Discussion Questions (opt.)

1. Who reminds us of what we've learned in this study?
2. What role does God's Word play in changing our thought patterns?
3. What does Philippians 4:9 tell us we should do?
4. What are some practical ways we can remember what we've learned in this study?
5. What will you do to keep learning?

Closing

Remind the class to plan some follow up steps to help them continue to learn. They can try some of the things listed in the Session 7 notes page or they can try something else.

Pray that the Spirit will continue to remind the members of what they have learned during this study. Pray that God will grant each member lasting victory in their thought patterns by continually relying on Him.

REFERENCES

Rydelnik, Michael, et al. "Ephesians 4:22-24". *The Moody Bible Commentary*. Chicago: Moody Press, 2014. Accessed 26 May 2018. Olive Tree Bible Software.

"SELF-CONDEMNATION." *What Does Self-condemnation Mean? Definition, Meaning and Pronunciation* (Free English Language Dictionary). N.p., n.d. Web. 03 Mar. 2016.

"Ownership." *American English Definition and Synonyms* | Macmillan Dictionary. N.p., n.d. Web. 03 Apr. 2016.

Nave, Orville J. "Entry for 'Ephod'". Naves Topical Bible Index. 1896. Accessed 3 April 2016. Olive Tree Bible Software.

Rydelnik, Michael, et al. "2 Samuel 30:7-8". *The Moody Bible Commentary*. Chicago: Moody Press, 2014. Accessed 3 April 2016. Olive Tree Bible Software.

Rydelnik, Michael, et al. "Ezekiel 28:11-19". *The Moody Bible Commentary*. Chicago: Moody Press, 2014. Accessed 9 April 2016. Olive Tree Bible Software.

Packer, J.I. "Is Satan Omnipresent?" *Christianity Today*. Christianity Today Mag., 19 Sept 2000. Web. Accessed 9 April 2016. <http://www.christianitytoday.com/ct/2000/september4/36.115.html >

Shirer, Priscilla. "Session 6: Helmet of Salvation." *Armor of God.* LifeWay Christian Resources, 07 Aug. 2015. Web. 26 Apr. 2016.

"legalism." *Merriam-Webster.com*. Merriam-Webster, 2011. Web. 17 Apr 2016.

McGee, Robert S. *The Search for Significance: Seeing Your True Worth Through God's Eyes.* Abridged Version. Thomas Nelson, Inc. 2012. Audible.

TerKeurst, Lysa. *Unglued: Making Wise Choices in the Midst of Raw Emotions.* Grand Rapids, MI: Zondervan, 2012. 7 Aug. 2012. Kindle.

"What are the different names of God and what do they mean?" Got Questions Ministries, n.d. Web. 24 Apr. 2016.

Rydelnik, Michael, et al. "2 Corinthians 12:1-8". *The Moody Bible Commentary*. Chicago: Moody Press, 2014. Accessed 1 February 2018. Olive Tree Bible Software.

Jones, Jay. "Compound Names of Jehovah." *Preaching Points*. N.p., 27 Aug. 2010. Web. 24 Apr. 2016.

Gerth, Holley. "What's True No Matter How We Feel." *You're Already Amazing Life Growth Guide: Embracing Who You Are, Becoming All God Created You To Be.* Grand Rapids, Michigan: Revell, 2016. 57. Print.

"unwholesome." *Merriam-Webster.com*. Merriam-Webster, 2011. Web. 4 Jun 2016.

"assume." *Merriam-Webster.com*. Merriam-Webster, 2011. Web. 4 Jun 2016.

"integrity." *Merriam-Webster.com*. Merriam-Webster, 2011. Web. 18 Jun 2016.

"noble." *Merriam-Webster.com*. Merriam-Webster, 2011. Web. 24 Apr 2016.

"praiseworthy." *Merriam-Webster.com*. Merriam-Webster, 2011. Web. 24 Apr 2016.

Visit Karen Baney online at:

Website: www.karenbaney.com

Facebook: www.fb.com/karenbaneybooks

Twitter: @karen_baney

Email: info@karenbaney.com

Fiction Books by Karen Baney

Prescott Pioneers Series:

A Dream Unfolding

A Heart Renewed

A Life Restored

A Hope Revealed

Hidden Prospects

Nickels: A Contemporary Novel

www.ingramcontent.com/pod-product-compliance
Lightning Source LLC
Chambersburg PA
CBHW062100090426

42741CB00015B/3294